ST. ANTHONY
Doctor of the Church

ST. ANTHONY
Doctor of the Church

BY SOPHRONIUS CLASEN O.F.M.

Translated from the German
by
IGNATIUS BRADY O.F.M.

FRANCISCAN HERALD PRESS

Chicago, Illinois 60609

ST. ANTHONY, DOCTOR OF THE CHURCH by Sophronius Clasen O.F.M., translated by Ignatius Brady O.F.M. from the German ANTONIUS, DIENER DES EVANGELIUMS UND DER KIRCHE, copyright ©1960 by Kuhlen Verlag, Monchengladbach, Germany. First and second English editions, 1961, Franciscan Herald Press, Chicago. Paperback editions 1973 and 1987. Copyright ©1973 by Franciscan Herald Press, 1434 West 51st Street, Chicago, Illinois 60609.

Library of Congress Cataloging-in-Publication Data

Clasen, Sophronius, 1909-
    St. Anthony, Doctor of the Church.

    Translation of: Antonius, Diener des Evangeliums und der Kirche.
    1. Anthony, of Padua, Saint, 1195-1231. 2. Christian saints—Italy—Biography. I. Title. II. Title: Saint Anthony, Doctor of the Church.
BX4700.A6C583 1987   282'.092'4 [B]   87-30311
ISBN 0-8199-0458-9 (pbk.)

CONTENTS

INTRODUCTION

"The repeated requests of my confreres," writes a Friar Minor shortly after the canonization of St. Anthony of Padua, "have urged me to undertake this work, so that I have finally deemed it good to narrate for his devoted clients and friends the life and deeds of Saint Anthony, to the honor and glory of Almighty God." When the Dietrich Coelde Press of Werl published my work, *Lehrer des Evangeliums (Doctor of the Gospel)*, in 1954, a book containing excerpts in German from the sermons of St. Anthony, many of my friends and confreres asked me to undertake a biography of this new Franciscan Doctor which would present his true spirit and character without recourse to the many legends which later grew up around him.

After fourteen years of study of the life and writings of the Saint, such a project seemed quite inviting. Yet there were, I thought, almost insurmountable difficulties in the way. One such difficulty arose from the question of chronology. The earliest details we have on the life of St. Anthony, in a work ascribed to Thomas of Pavia O.F.M. (d. 1280), follow a strict chronological course up to the year 1222; then they pass over some eight years, to treat of events which happened between 1230 and the canonization in 1232. As a result, we know little about the Saint's extensive activity as a preacher in upper Italy and almost nothing of his work in southern France. All other sources of the life of

Anthony from the thirteenth century, namely, Julian of Speyer O.F.M. (before 1235), the *Dialogue on the Life of the Holy Friars Minor* (about 1245), Raymond of Saint-Romain O.F.M. (d. 1287), the *Florentine Legend* (about 1300), and also the Legend *Benignitas* which dates from the early fourteenth century, are merely expansions and revisions of the first Life of St. Anthony and offer no help in filling in the gaps of his history. The first to deal with Anthony's work in France is John Rigauld O.F.M., in the early fourteenth century. Yet the value of his account is lessened by the fact that the tendency to add legendary details, already evident at times in some of the pieces from the thirteenth century, finds full expression. This is even more true of the *Book of Miracles* (1367-1374), since of the sixty-five miracles recounted in it only forty-one come from earlier sources while the other twenty-four are proper to this collection. Similarly, Bartholomew of Pisa O.F.M. in 1385 gathered together without rhyme or reason all he could find on St. Anthony. In these later documents, we must not expect to meet the real St. Anthony, but rather the Wonderworker surrounded by countless legends—a figure in complete opposition to a sermon of the Saint in which he cites St. Gregory the Great: *In the time of the Apostles miracles took place for the conversion of the unbelievers, but in our days such wonders have ceased; for we too water a newly planted tree only until such time as it can draw its nourishment by itself from the earth.* Faced with this fact of history, we should let St. Anthony himself speak to us as much as possible in his own sermons.

In keeping with the modern penchant for pictures, we have endeavored to illustrate our text with photographs of every place where St. Anthony lived and worked. Special thanks is due to Mr. Bruno Geuter, of Mönchengladbach, who has supplied by his own work and travels the greater part of the photos and has thereby given new life to the old biographies. His task also encountered difficulties. Some of the places intimately bound up with the life of St. Anthony have suffered from the ravages of time (beside natural catastrophes, we have only to think of wars and of persecutions, which were often followed by the destruction of monasteries and friaries in Portugal, France, and Italy); or they have been so changed in structure in the course of more than seven hundred years, that in their present condition they contribute but little to a biography such as this.

Another difficulty, by no means the least, lies in the fact that Anthony labored in widely scattered lands. The great son of Portugal was first a missionary in Morocco, then came by way of Sicily to upper Italy, worked later in France and again in northern Italy, where he finally died at Padua. But since the author of this biography is a religious, he could not personally visit all places where the Saint had lived. Hence the pictures had to be planned ahead of time for the photographers, according to a tentative sketch of his life; others were sought at the cost of great efforts from photographers of the different countries. In particular, the writer feels deeply indebted to the Very Reverend Father Provincial of Toulouse, who so graciously allowed a confrere of the author, Father Fidelis Durieux, to act as companion and guide to Mr. Geuter in his quest of Franciscan places connected with St. Anthony's sojourn in France.

Anyhow, our account and the pictures are meant to supplement each other in unfolding the life of St. Anthony as it actually ran its course. The author can well make his own the words which Thomas of Pavia wrote of himself: "I truly feel entirely inadequate for such a task. If nonetheless I venture to write, I do so in the hope that he who knows what my heart would like to say will bring my project to a good end."

Mönchengladbach, Feast of Saint Anthony of Padua, 1959

ST. ANTHONY
Doctor of the Church

PORTUGAL'S NOBLE SON

Ere the sun, which in early morning breaks forth upon the city of Lisbon, sinks at evening in the west behind the far bank of the wide Tagus, it once more sheds the full splendor of its light upon the city. So too did the Saint, who in Italy is simply called "Il Santo," take his rise in Lisbon; and before his mortal life ended in an early death, he cast new lustre on his native city and through the brilliance of his sanctity gave to her a new and undying glory.

The kingdom of Portugal, born, so to speak, on the very field of battle in the midst of crusades against the Saracens, no longer enjoyed its original glory at that time. Count Afonso Henriques, the Conqueror, had assumed leadership and the title of king in the year 1139, immediately after the victorious battle over the Moors at Ourique (Southern Portugal). To free himself from all fealty to the king of Castile, he offered his kingdom some five years later to the Church, declaring himself a vassal of the pope. In October 1147, with the help of Dutch and English crusaders, he was able to drive the Moors from Lisbon (which in 1256 became the capital of the kingdom). In 1179, Pope Alexander III confirmed Afonso in his royal dignity, while the king on his part showed his loyalty to the Church and the pope by the many benefits he bestowed on the Church and the many monasteries which he founded.

When Sancho I succeeded him on the throne of Portugal

in 1185, the kingdom was soon troubled by difficulties with the nobles and the Church. Like his contemporary Philip Augustus of France, Sancho was a man of unbridled passions and anything but a devoted son of the Church and loyal vassal of the Apostolic See. In his endeavor to fill the royal coffers and build many great castles, he relied on the support of the ordinary people, and had little to do with the nobility or the higher clergy of the land. At the same time, he had an exaggerated notion of his royal dignity and absolute independence, which led him to think the Church possessed far too much wealth and political power and to consider the yoke of St. Peter far too oppressive. Such an attitude soon made this vassal of the pope a bitter enemy of the Church. And because he had moved his family and court to the Alcázar at Coimbra, he was soon in constant strife with the bishop of that city. After 1208 this discord broke out into open conflict, and brought down on the king the punishments of Innocent III, his liege-lord.

FOUNDED ON GOD

"As the morning-star in the midst of the clouds," writes one of Anthony's early biographers, "the future Saint shone in this world. But, as the Gospel tells us, a tree is known by its fruits and the plant by its roots. So too were his parents, like those of John the Baptist, just before God, walking blamelessly in all the commandments and ordinances of the Lord." Fourteenth-century accounts give their names as Martin and Maria. When still later writers tell us that their family name was Bulhom and find a relationship to Godfrey of Bouillon, the Crusader, who became the first king of Jerusalem, we can only conclude that such fabrications were intended to give our great Saint the noblest genealogy possible and so increase his claim on our veneration. Nonetheless, we are sure that his parents belonged to the more

4

important families of the city, in fact, to the nobility which rendered loyal service to the king and had shown a truly knightly spirit and courage in the wars of liberation. They possessed a house in keeping with their station, just west of the cathedral of the city, quite close to its main doors. Here our Saint was born to them in 1195. He was, the biographers tell us, their first child; and the young couple, aware of their great responsibility as parents, sought from the first to impart to him their own deep religious faith and noble spirit.

The house was transformed already in the thirteenth century into a church called Santo Antonio da Sé. When this was destroyed by an earthquake and fire on November 1, 1755, it was completely rebuilt in the form it has today. The room in which the great son of Portugal first saw the light of day formed the crypt under the church; it was later converted into the present simple chapel. Above the altar of this tiny oratory, a marble tablet tells us that here a great Saint of God began his mortal life: "In this house, according to the testimony of our forefathers, was born Anthony, who has been transported from this earth to the celestial mansions on high."

A few days after the birth of their first-born son and heir, the young parents brought him to the nearby cathedral for holy baptism. At the sacred font he received the name of Ferdinand (Fernando).

His baptismal church, usually called the Sé Patriarcal, is dedicated to our Lady; and, thanks to the gift of King Afonso, since 1173 it has been the resting place of the relics of St. Vincent, the great Spanish martyr. Located in the medieval part of Lisbon, it lies at the foot of the Castle São Jorge, which overlooks the entire city and harbor, and which from the days of the Romans, Goths, and Moors, had served as the fortress and guardian of the town. The church is one of the typical medieval buildings of the old

5

city, going back to the year 1147, when Lisbon was liberated from the hands of the Moors. Old traditions say that King Afonso the Conqueror began its construction on the spot occupied earlier by a great Moorish mosque. Its powerful west façade with its two striking towers (the one to the left containing the baptistery) is built in Romanesque style, while the church itself has three wide Gothic aisles. In the middle of the baptistery still stands the ancient and venerable font at which the child Ferdinand received the waters of regeneration and of life and became a child of God. Here too we find an inscription reminding visitors of this important fact of our Saint's life: "Here the waters of holy baptism cleansed Anthony from all stain of original sin. The whole world rejoices in his light, Padua in his body, heaven in his soul."

When the waters of baptism touch the body, by the power of the Holy Spirit they cleanse the soul of all sin. He descends upon the one baptized, to change the child of wrath into a child of grace.

The grace of baptism, the Saint said later, *which a man receives in holy baptism, is symbolized by two things which the priest presents to the neophyte: the white garment and the burning candle. The white garment is the sign of the innocence which baptism has bestowed, while the light typifies the life of virtue he should lead. But man loses these when he besmirches the white garment by sin and so extinguishes the burning candle.* Since St. Anthony had such a vivid appreciation of the Christian's dignity as a child of God, it should not surprise us that later biographers delighted to portray the noble manners and chivalrous conduct of the youthful Ferdinand (though we really know nothing of his childhood). His parents surely implanted in him a deep piety and nobleness of mind. Therefore, we are told, he kept himself from the frivolous ways of youth and imitated the good example of his parents. He was ever eager

6

to help the poor and needy, since from childhood he had a great sympathy for the sufferings of others. He often visited churches and monasteries, and what he there learned of the truths of the Faith he did not forget, but "stored them in the little treasure-chest of his heart."

His parents soon sent him to the cathedral school of his native city, which Bishop Suger of Lisbon maintained and directed in the rooms adjacent to the cloister of the church. Here he learned the rudiments of Latin and received a solid training in the doctrines of faith and morals. Here too, as a boy in school, he felt the first signs of a vocation to the priesthood. Later, Bishop Suger II Viegas, who succeeded Suger I as bishop in 1209, was to give testimony on the early years of Ferdinand's life, and say that it was a good omen for his later life as a servant of the Gospel and the Church that his parents permitted their son to be trained by the ministers of Christ in this school.

While still in school, the youthful Ferdinand would hardly have escaped the temptations that come to all adolescents. Yet the more the world and the flesh called to him, the firmer grew his determination to devote his life entirely to God and to please him alone. In the shadow of the cathedral, to which the pious Portuguese came in pilgrimage because it was dedicated to the Mother of God, he felt the power of her intercession, and all his life he had recourse to her protection and help in all needs and difficulties. With her assistance he was able to preserve unsullied in soul and body till his glorious death the shining white garment of a child of God.

Our Lady's name is a strong tower. To her the sinner has recourse, and there finds security and salvation. O sweet name, which gives the sinner strength and blessed hope. We pray you, our Lady, Star of the Sea, shine upon us in our distress on the sea of life, and lead us to safe harbor and the ineffable joys of eternity.

Until his fifteenth year Ferdinand remained at home with his parents, and then left only to answer the call of God. The older he grew, the more he withdrew from his companions, at least in spirit, since for them King Sancho with his scandalous way of living became their idol and hero who promised them riches and pleasures and counted on their support in his many wars and battles. If at times Ferdinand himself felt the temptation to imitate them, he had only to think that such a life would separate him from God in order to regain his inner determination to leave it all. No matter how bright the hopes and prospects might be that the king or the whole world could offer him, they held no attraction for him when they were compared to God. He grew more and more determined to abandon everything here on earth that could hinder him on the path to God, and to leave his friends and schoolmates, whose sole desire seemed to be for money and good times. He soon carried out his resolution, gave up his inheritance, left home and family, and entered the monastery of São Vicente de Fora (so called because it was then located "without the walls of the city"), to receive the religious habit of St. Augustine. This happened, it would seem, in the year 1210. At São Vicente the canons followed the rule of the great Doctor, Augustine, a rule which combines the personal sanctification of the individual with a monastic type of community life, and through the practice of individual poverty and common ownership seeks to foster mutual love among its followers. Ferdinand took this decisive step with the firm determination of making it a means to die to the world and to live for God alone. *Whoever enters a monastery,* he wrote later, *goes so to speak to his grave. Yet the grace of the Holy Spirit gives strength to the weak, makes light and easy all that is difficult, and by the balm of his love turns*

8

to sweetness all that is bitter; for, he who loves, knows naught that is hard for him.

The ancient priory or monastery of São Vicente, which perished with the cell of Ferdinand in an earthquake in 1755, was founded by King Afonso I soon after the conquest of Lisbon and made subject to the monastery in the capital city of Coimbra. As a royal foundation it was richly endowed, but Ferdinand was soon to realize, as did Francis of Assisi, that without arms a rich monastery can defend itself only with difficulty against the encroachments of the mighty and powerful of this world. This monastery, with many others, was involved in the crown's quarrels with the Church, especially after 1211 when Afonso II, eldest son of King Sancho and persistent enemy of the Bishop of Porto, ascended the throne of Portugal.

Ferdinand soon had another source of distraction. More often than he desired, his old friends came to the door of the priory and by their vehement discussions on politics disturbed that monastic peace which for him was a prime requisite for quiet study and so important as a suitable preparation for the reception of Holy Orders. Often he must have thought of the famous dictum of the great doctor St. Jerome, that he does not deserve praise who seeks Jerusalem, but he who there lives an exemplary life. After he had studied some two years at the Augustinian convent in Lisbon, Ferdinand made the firm resolve to leave his home town. One drawback to such a decision was his vow which bound him to the priory of São Vicente; but when his superiors learned of his determination, they agreed, even if unwillingly, to let him transfer to the monastery of the order at Coimbra.

Coimbra is situated about a hundred miles north of Lisbon, on a hill along the Mondego River. It was the capital of the kingdom of Portugal and the seat of a bishop, while the archbishop of Portugal resided at Braga. Since

1131 the Augustinian Canons had had their principal convent in this city. Here Canon John, who had once been a student and master at the University of Paris, instructed the young clerics and prepared them for the priesthood. Though the University, which was to make Coimbra famous throughout the world, was founded only later, the city was already well known because of the flourishing school of the sons of St. Augustine. Here, after 1212, young Ferdinand continued his preparation for Sacred Orders. His old biographers tell us that in his study of Sacred Scripture, which formed the heart of theology, he sought first the literal sense of the Scriptures; and then, through the spiritual sense, he endeavored to come to a deeper understanding of the truths of our faith and their meaning for Christian living. In this he was not a hearer only but a doer of the word, meditating on what he learned and applying to himself first of all what he knew to be right and true. He found such joy in studies that he zealously devoted himself to them both day and night. At Coimbra, too, he gave particular attention to the controversies and heresies of his day, to acquire a strong and unshakeable conviction in matters of faith, before he would go out to preach to others. Besides Holy Scripture, he examined likewise the second source of Christian faith, that is, tradition, immersing himself, like a good Augustinian, in the writings and teaching of his patron, St. Augustine. Whatever he read, of Scripture, of Augustine, of the other Fathers of the Church, he impressed so deeply on his memory that later in his priestly activity he could draw on such knowledge at will. Little wonder then that we are told that his astounding memory was as valuable to him as books to others. The convent of the Augustinians at Coimbra was dedicated to the Holy Cross, and therefore called "Santa Cruz." Inspired by this title, Ferdinand grew to have a great love for the Cross and for Christ Crucified. It was here too that

10

he shared in the triumph of the Holy Cross, when, after the tremendous victory of the Christians over the Moors at Las Navas de Tolosa, July 16, 1212, Queen Urraca of Portugal, the consort of Afonso II and sister of the victor, Alfonso VIII of Castile, came to the church of Santa Cruz to give thanks to Christ Crucified for the divine assistance that had won the battle. Not only had her brother won the victory under the banner of the Cross, but she knew too that this victory was due to the prayers and solemn processions which Innocent III and his household had held in honor of the Holy Cross. Such love of the Cross and the Crucified was to link Ferdinand the more closely to the Seraphic Saint of Assisi, who had bidden his friars to pray: "We adore you, O Lord Jesus Christ, here and in all the churches which are in the whole world, and we bless you because by your holy Cross you have redeemed the world."

Like a wise architect, Ferdinand thus laid a solid foundation for his later life in these nine years of study at Coimbra. They were not always peaceful years, for Anthony found himself more than once sharing in the sufferings of Calvary! True peace can hardly thrive where injustice, strife, and sin abound. When Afonso II had come to the throne of Portugal in 1211, the country breathed a sigh of relief, in the hope that the trouble between Church and State would now be ended. All such hope soon vanished, however, since the king was engaged in a constant struggle with his sister, whom he had cheated out of her inheritance. Though some of the nobles adhered to the unjust monarch, the two bishops, who had been appointed by King Sancho as executors of his will, excommunicated the new ruler and laid his land under interdict. In addition, the king of nearby Léon, who was the protector of Afonso's brother Don Pedro, interfered on behalf of the latter. The situation became at last so hopelessly entangled that Afonso sent urgent appeals to his liege lord, Innocent III, to act as

11

arbiter. Because of political developments and the venality of the papal legates, however, the crafty king succeeded for years in maintaining his unjust position and even in intimidating his opponents among the clergy by ecclesiastical punishments, until at last the whole story of his deceitfulness became public.

The king was not the only one who feared neither excommunication and interdict nor the judgment of God. Some of the higher clergy were also involved, and merited the severe reproach of Honorius III (who had meanwhile succeeded Innocent III). In 1220 he wrote: "Because all of them go their own way and care only for their own interests, to their own damnation will they seek in vain to excuse themselves at the marriage feast of the Eternal King. Even priests of the altar of God speak openly like Sodom of old of their sins and thus become a scandal and occasion of ruin to their faithful. There is scarcely anyone who sets himself like a strong wall to protect the house of God." Such reproaches, unfortunately, were well merited by Bishop Peter of Coimbra and Prior John of Santa Cruz. The bishop had been told by Honorius III that he was a hireling and not a shepherd of his flock, because he had sided with the king against his archbishop and the Church of Christ, and had feared a weak man rather than God. The other partisan of the king had already been accused before Innocent III of squandering the goods of the monastery, and had been excommunicated as a result. However, he completely ignored the punishment and insolently continued to exercise his priestly office; and by this open contumacy, he made himself morally suspect. He did indeed withdraw into solitude shortly before the death of Innocent III; but after the pope had died, the unscrupulous prior boldly returned to his former post. Hence Honorius III called for an investigation into the whole affair.

As a result of these sad conditions, the canons of Santa

Cruz found themselves split into two factions. One group sided with the prior, currying his favor for their own interests; the others, Ferdinand among them, looked to Master John, whom they charged to present their complaints before the judges of the ecclesiastical inquisition. Ferdinand was no longer in Coimbra when the investigation was completed, but the memory of that sad time seems to have lived on in him, for he wrote at a later date: *The wicked have wrought upon my back, says the Prophet. The wicked superior beats upon the back, that is, the patience, of his subject. To the superior such persecution brings ruin, but to the subject an eternal reward. The devil crushes man like grapes in a wine-press through trials and tribulations, that the good like good wine may be saved in the cellars of eternal life, while the wicked like bad grapes are cast forth like leavings to eternal damnation.* If the memory of such bitter days and the anguish of soul they had cost him remained fixed in his memory, Anthony also recalled the solace and strength he then found in meditation on his crucified Lord: *With his arms outstretched upon the Cross, Christ covers as with wings all who have recourse to him, and hides them from the wrath of the wicked one in his sacred wounds. Let us lift up our eyes to him! Let us gaze upon the author of our salvation, Jesus! Let us consider how our Lord hung upon the Cross and was nailed to it!*

If Ferdinand had not nourished in himself a love of purity, of poverty, and of self-denial, God's Providence would not have found in him a wondrous tool for its wise designs!

POOR WITH THE POVERELLO OF ASSISI

The hour of God's Providence came for Ferdinand at Santa Cruz when Don Pedro, adversary and brother of King Afonso, gave to this monastery the bones of the

13

Protomartyrs of the young Franciscan Order (Berard, Peter, Adjutus, Accursius, and Otto). He had brought them back with him from Morocco and given them to his friend, the Augustinian Canon John Roberti at Coimbra. They were now carried in solemn procession—in the presence of Queen Urraca and a great crowd of people—to the cloister of the monastery and there laid to rest. As Ferdinand on this occasion heard of the wonders that God had wrought through them, he was filled with holy envy and said within himself: "Oh, if the Most High would but let me share the crown of his holy martyrs! Oh, if only I too might kneel and feel upon my neck for the Name of Jesus the sword of the executioner! I wonder if this will ever happen to me? Is it possible that I too could look forward to such a happy death?" As these thoughts stirred within him, they gave him no peace, for had not these friars started their journey to martyrdom from this very country? He was determined to follow in their footsteps, and at once sought a way to carry out his plan.

In the year 1217 Francis had sent his friars into many lands, and it was then that they came for the first time to Portugal. But because they were strange-looking men, barefoot, and poorly clad, the people did not receive them for fear that they might be some kind of heretics. Their mission would have ended in disaster had not pious women of the royal house taken them under their protection. Queen Urraca became their friend and gave them a small church at Coimbra, while Sancia, the sister of her consort, did the same at Alenquer, north of Lisbon.

It was at the friary of Alenquer that Berard and his companions stopped in 1219, after Francis at the wish of Honorius III had sent them forth from the Chapter as missionaries to the Saracens. Later, when they attempted to preach in the mosque at Seville, they almost gained martyrdom at the hands of the enraged local Sultan; but he relented, and allowed them to pass over to Morocco. Here they soon went to the open market-place; and Berard, who could speak the language, mounted a wagon and without further ado began to preach the Gospel of Christ and to refute the religion of the Mohammedans. He and his companions were instantly seized and cast into prison. Later the group was handed over to some Christians, with orders to return them to their own land. When the Christians released them, the friars returned to preach. This happened several times, until the Sultan in high dudgeon had them tortured and, seeing their steadfastness, at last had them beheaded. When Francis heard of their glorious death, he exclaimed: "Now at last I have in truth five friars!" Then he must have raised his eyes to heaven and blessed the friary of Alenquer, from which the martyrs had started out, with the words: "Holy town and convent, be you blest, for through the holy martyrdom of these brothers you have offered to God rich and precious flowers, the first fruits of the Friars Minor, who now possess the happiness of heaven. May you ever have perfect friars within your walls, friars who will follow faithfully the way of the holy Gospel!"

The bones of the glorious martyrs of the young Franciscan Order rested in the cloister of Santa Cruz until they were enclosed later in a precious silver reliquary. But, as for Ferdinand, he waited impatiently for the day when the confreres of these martyrs would come once more to the monastery. The very contrast between the holy and exemplary life of these simple men and the sad state of affairs in the priory must have stirred up anew in him the longing which even Coimbra had not fulfilled, to give himself unreservedly to God and to belong, body and soul, to him alone. For, his first biographer remarks that when he met the Franciscans he saw that, though they possessed no training in theology, they showed in their entire deportment the power of the deepest knowledge of God. Their simple house, with the church that Queen Urraca had given them, lay on a hillside not far from Coimbra; and it was called Santo Antonio dos Olivais, because the church was dedicated to Saint Anthony the Abbot and was surrounded by olive groves.

When finally the friars on their quest for alms knocked at the door of the priory, Ferdinand made use of the occasion to speak to them and reveal his desires: "Dear Brothers, I would gladly put on the habit of your order if only you would promise to send me as soon as possible to the land of the Saracens, that I might gain the crown of the holy martyrs." In their simplicity the friars were most happy at his request, and immediately agreed to receive him two days later, lest his resolution might suffer through delay.

While the friars returned to their house, Ferdinand went to the prior of the monastery to ask his consent. Once again his vow of stability which attached him to the priory stood in the way of his desires. Santa Cruz, moreover, possessed a special papal privilege according to which "none of the brethren after making profession of the vows of the order could leave the monastery without the consent of the prior and the whole community; nor could any other order receive a canon who had left the priory without a special written authorization."

Because Ferdinand was generally held in high regard in the priory as an earnest and loveable religious, it was only with great difficulty that he could get the prior to give his consent. But at last the opposition of the prior (who was under excommunication at the time!) gave way before the holy ardor of Ferdinand. When it came time for Ferdinand to take leave of his confreres, one of the partisans of the prior could not restrain his resentment against him any longer and indirectly accused him of inconstancy by calling after him in irony: "Go now, go! Now you will surely

16

become a saint!" With ready wit but deeper humility Ferdinand gave him this answer: "When you hear that I have become a saint, then give praise to God!" With that, Ferdinand accompanied the Brothers of St. Francis to the little house of Santo Antonio dos Olivais, where he was clothed with the poor habit of a Friar Minor and joyfully received into the little community, to dwell with them in their poor huts near the chapel of St. Anthony and to live a life poor in goods but rich in the things of God. At his clothing he asked the superiors that henceforth he might be called Anthony after the patron of their church. He did this with a certain foresight and love of solitude, because he wished in this way to hide himself from any search on the part of his relatives and, under a new name, to avoid the importunities of his friends.

This took place in the summer of 1220. Since it was only on September 22 of that year that Honorius III made the novitiate obligatory for the Franciscan Order, Anthony was enrolled in the order and made profession at the time of his clothing. He remained for some time with the friars in Coimbra, to learn from them the meaning of the Franciscan life and rule and to acquire the spirit of Franciscan poverty, chastity, and obedience.

The people of Sion, of whom the prophet Isaias speaks, are the poor in spirit, because, lifted up above all things of earth, they stand upon the high towers of their poor life and contemplate the Son of God who was a stranger on earth and is now glorified in the heavenly fatherland. The Lord comforts Sion, because he comforts with his graces all who find no comfort in earthly riches. Hence we read: The Lord will comfort all the ruins of Sion. Only when the proud house of earthly comfort is reduced to a ruin can the Lord prepare a dwelling place for his inward comforting. Her wilderness shall become a garden of the Lord, for out of the desert of outward poverty the Lord makes a garden full of inward delights.

MISSIONARY TO MOROCCO

Anthony's burning zeal for the Faith and his intense desire for martyrdom did not let him rest long at Coimbra. Soon after his entrance into the Franciscan Order he besought the minister provincial for the permission and obedience to go among the infidels, which the friars had promised him earlier. He wanted to preach Christ openly to the unbelievers; he desired to offer himself as a witness to the truth of the Christian Faith among them; he longed to be a victim for Christ who sacrificed himself for our sake on the altar of the Cross.

Anthony was thus taking part in a new crusade. At a time when selfish or nationalist interests had dulled men's zeal for armed combat against the infidels, Honorius III called upon Christendom (especially during the course of 1219) to send messengers of the Gospel of Christ among the Saracens, holy priests who "would persevere in patience and long for martyrdom and willingly expose themselves to danger, and with joyful heart praise God if for his Name's sake they should suffer a martyr's death."

"If the friars wish to go among the Saracens or other unbelievers," wrote Francis in answer to this plea of the pope, "they may go with the permission of their minister and servant. If the minister judges them fit to be sent, he should give them permission and not refuse them; for he shall be held to render an account to the Lord, should he act indiscreetly in this or in other things. The friars who go, can fulfill their spiritual mission among the infidels in two ways. The first is this: not to engage in strife and controversy, but to be subject to every human creature for God's sake, and simply confess that they are Christians.

The other way is this, that, should they see it pleases God, they announce the word of God: that they must believe in Almighty God, Father and Son and Holy Spirit, the Creator of all things; and in the Son, the Redeemer and Savior; and that they must be baptized and be made Christians, because unless a man be born again of water and the Holy Spirit, he cannot enter into the kingdom of God. Such things and others, as it shall please the Lord, they can say to them and to others. For the Lord says in the Gospel: Everyone who acknowledges me before men, I also will acknowledge him before my Father in heaven; and whoever is ashamed of me and my words, of him will the Son of Man be ashamed when he comes in his glory and that of the Father and of the holy angels. And let all the friars remember that they have surrendered themselves in soul and body to our Lord Jesus Christ and must for love of him expose themselves to enemies visible and invisible, because the Lord says: He who loses his life for my sake will save it unto life everlasting. Blessed are those who suffer persecution for justice' sake, for theirs is the kingdom of heaven. If they have persecuted me, they will persecute you also. If they persecute you in one town, flee to another. Blessed are you when men hate you and reproach you and shut you out and reject your name as evil and, speaking falsely, say all manner of evil against you, for my sake. Rejoice in that day and exult, because your reward is great in heaven. But I say to you, my friends: Do not be terrified by these things, and do not be afraid of those who kill the body, and after that have nothing more that they can do. Take care you do not become alarmed. For by your patience you will win your souls. But he who has persevered to the end will be saved." Once he had come to Morocco, Anthony was soon besieged by a severe illness, which kept him confined to a sick-bed until the spring of 1221.

SERVANT OF THE GOSPEL
AND THE CHURCH

ITALY'S GREAT PREACHER

Sick and exhausted, Anthony boarded a ship which was to take him back to his homeland. But once again God's Providence had other plans for him; for the ship ran into stormy weather and fought in vain against the sea and adverse winds. Instead of making anchor in the safety of a Portuguese port, it was driven to the east coast of Sicily, south of Messina.

The Friars Minor in that town lovingly received their sick brother, even though he was unknown to them, and nursed him back to health, mindful of the words of their Seraphic Father: "If any friar falls sick, the other friars are not to leave him, no matter where he may be, without appointing one of the friars, or more, if need be, who will take such care of him as they would wish to have themselves." But since Francis continues: "And I ask the friar who is sick to give thanks to the Creator for all things, and to desire to be whatever God wills for him, whether healthy or sick," Anthony joyfully obeyed. As he had long since let himself be led by God's will in all the dangers of his life, so now in the days of his illness he offered his will to that of the Creator, knowing that submission to the will of God is the proof of true virtue: *It is only in adversity that we come to know whether we have made real progress in goodness.*

Led by God into Solitude

At Messina Anthony learned from the friars that the Chapter of Pentecost would be held for all the friars at the Porziuncola on May 30, 1221. Although he was weak and still felt the effects of his illness, he made his way with the other friars to the far-off region of Umbria.

Today the plain below the hill-town of Assisi—the home-town of the Little Poor Man Francis—is occupied by a great basilica which shelters beneath its towering dome a poor little chapel. At the time of the chapter of 1221, it was only this little church of "St. Mary of the Angels," the Porziuncola as it is called, that stood there surrounded by trees and huts. Then as now, it was an object of affection, for it was the cradle of the Franciscan Order. Here, on the feast of St. Mathias in 1208 or 1209, God revealed to Francis his future way of life. He was to live like the Apostles and possess neither gold nor silver nor money, to have neither purse nor wallet nor bread nor even a staff for the way, to wear neither shoes nor two tunics, but to go forth to preach the kingdom of God and call men to penance. Some years later the Benedictines of Monte Subasio near Assisi gave him this little church, and from that time it became the center of the order. Around it the friars put up little huts of mud and wattles, and they convened there for their chapters.

Among the three thousand or more friars who gathered there in 1221 from all over the world, Anthony found himself unknown and alone. He knew no one, and none knew him or asked about his origin or country. This did not trouble him, for he did his best to hide himself among the many brothers, anticipating what he was to write later: *Let us act like some beggars do when they seek alms: for they hide their good clothes and appear in tatters. So let us too hide what good we have, and show only the misery of our*

21

guilt and our infirmity, that the Lord may give us the alms of his graces. At this chapter Anthony saw St. Francis for the first time; but he did not hear him speak, since Francis, who was sick, made use of Brother Elias as his spokesman when he had something to say to the friars about their way of life. Francis does not seem to have met Anthony, or to have had any inkling of his future greatness. His attention was taken up by many problems; and the individual friars with whom he conversed were men who were already outstanding for their humility, and spirit of prayer and penance.

When, finally, the chapter came to an end and the ministers provincial and the friars entrusted to them made ready to leave for their respective territories, Anthony suddenly found himself without a place to go. An unknown newcomer among so many brethren, and apparently of little use, he had not caught the eye of any of the provincials. It was then that he humbly approached Friar Gratian, who had been appointed minister of the province of upper Italy, and diffidently asked him if he would request the minister general to assign him to his province, and if he would take him along to Romagna and there instruct him in the life and ways of the order. He made no mention in his request of his background or his years of study or his knowledge of theology. Instead, for love of the lowly and humble Savior, he hid his great talents; for, he was determined to know nothing else or long for and love naught else save Jesus Christ and him crucified. Brother Gratian found something attractive in this unassuming friar and took him with him.

Thus it was that Anthony came to northern Italy. At his request, Gratian sent him to the little hermitage at Montepaolo, which lay near the city of Forlì. There, far from the noise of the world, Anthony was for the time being to live for God alone. Since his order combined both the active and the contemplative life, there were many holy friars in those days who led a life of contemplation in complete

22

seclusion from the world. This was indeed the mind of St. Francis, who himself would go off from time to time to spend weeks in solitude and who rejoiced at being told of the friars in Spain: "In our land, your friars at a little hermitage have so arranged their way of living that one half of them takes care of the needs of the house, while the other half gives itself to contemplation. Then each week they change places, and those who had been active become contemplatives, while the others turn to the work of the friary."

The Franciscan place at Montepaolo was such a hermitage, with a poor farmhouse which some kind folk had given them to serve as their simple abode. After all these centuries, of course, nothing remains today of the old building. In its place there is a newer house and barn, while close by is a little chapel, constructed of the stones of the older building, in memory of Anthony's sojourn there.

A man of prayer and penance like St. Francis, Anthony shared his love of the solitary life and the freedom it gave him for communion with God. Hence he treasured the time he could spend in this way as a precious gift of God, given to him that in quiet and silence he might learn humility of heart, and in prayer, meditation, and penitential practices acquire that rich inner fulness which he would later pour forth into the souls of others.

The rule he followed was that which Francis himself had drawn up for religious life in a hermitage: "Those friars who wish to live as religious in hermitages should be three or at most four in number. Two of them shall be the mothers and two or at least one shall be the sons. The first two shall live the life of Martha, and the other two the life of Mary Magdalen. The two who are mothers shall lead the life of Martha, and the two sons shall lead the life of Mary and shall have an enclosure in which each can have a cell of his own in which he will pray and sleep. And let them pray

Compline of the day at the moment when the sun is setting, and they shall endeavor to keep silence; and they shall say their Hours of the Office, get up at the time of Matins, and seek first the kingdom of God and his justice. And at the proper hour they shall say Prime, and after Tierce they may break silence and can go and speak with their mothers, and, if they wish, they may ask of them an alms for the love of the Lord God, like other poor people. And afterwards, at the time appointed, let them say Sext and None and Vespers. And they must not permit any person to enter the enclosure where they live, or eat there. But those friars who are the mothers shall be solicitous to keep themselves away from every one, and in obedience to their minister they shall protect their sons from all people, so that none may speak with them. And these sons are not to speak with any person except their mothers and with their minister and custos, whenever it shall please these to visit them with the blessing of God. The sons moreover shall sometimes assume the duties of the mothers whenever they shall find it mutually good to do so for a time. Let them carefully and exactly observe all that has been said above."

At Montepaolo Anthony followed to the letter these regulations of the Seraphic Father. Since he was to live the "life of Mary Magdalen" and saw that one friar had made himself a cell in a nearby cave for his own days of solitude, Anthony earnestly besought him to let him make use of it, since it was well suited for quiet and lonely prayer. The friar acceded to the wishes of his young confrere, and thereafter each morning saw Anthony, after the Chapter of Prime or at the end of Tierce, betake himself with a morsel of bread and a jug of water to this damp grotto, there in great severity and penance and interior prayer to live for God alone and give himself completely to love for him. There he would pray (as was said of Francis) to his heavenly Father and call upon the eternal Judge for mercy, or he would speak with Christ as with a friend and earnestly plead for all the faithful and especially for sinners. Such was the manner in which he spent the days, in solitude and penance, forcing his body to be subject to his spirit, and returning to the little community only for the canonical Hours of Office as the order of the day required. In his great zeal he exhausted his weak health by fasting and vigils, so that one day when the bell summoned him to rejoin the community he was so weak and trembling that he almost collapsed. It was only with the help of two of his confreres that he was able to return to the hermitage.

The contemplative man goes his way alone, keeps himself far from the restless throng, and lives in the sorrow of penance. He seeks solitude for body and soul.

When Anthony saw how the other friars, when they had finished their prayers, often did various manual tasks about the house to help the community, he reproached himself for being a useless servant who did not deserve the bread he ate and left to others the work required for community life while he sought his own interests alone. He recalled to mind that Christ had come not to be served but to serve, and that Francis had bidden his friars: "And let one unhesitatingly reveal his needs to the other, that the latter may find and provide what is necessary for him. And let each love and cherish his brother as a mother loves and cherishes her child, in those things in which God shall give them grace." Full of humility he went to the Father Guardian and on bended knee asked for permission to clean the pots and pans in the kitchen and sweep the corridors and cells. This humble work he performed with unusual devotion and care, and he now felt satisfied that he could eat his bread with a clear conscience. *One and the same love embraces both God and neighbor, and this love is the Holy Spirit, for God is love.*

25

Placed like a Lamp on the Lamp-stand

In the summer of 1222 the provincial, Friar Gratian, sent some of the brethren from various convents to Forlì, to be ordained there to the sacred priesthood. Bishop Ricciardellus Belmonti of Forlì conferred this sacrament in the old church of San Mercuriale, which had been rebuilt in 1176 after a disastrous fire and dedicated to the first bishop and saint of the town. Along with clerics from St. Dominic's Order of Preachers, a group of the sons of St. Francis also received Holy Orders. "Among these," says the first biographer, "was Anthony."

According to this account, then, it was only in 1222 that Anthony was ordained a priest. Many later writers, it is true, believed that Anthony was promoted to the priesthood at Coimbra, while he was still an Augustinian Canon and hence before his entry into the Franciscan Order. Yet church law at that time did not permit anyone to be ordained before he had completed his thirtieth year of age, and only in cases of actual necessity could a man be ordained at the age of twenty five. Such a necessity would more readily be found in the tiny friary of the Franciscans who had so few priests than in the great Augustinian foundation at Coimbra.

Afterwards the participants in this solemn ceremony gathered in the refectory of the Dominican convent for a simple meal. Here the minister provincial suggested that in place of the usual table-reading one of the friars should give a short sermon for the edification of all present. But one after the other declined, claiming he was unprepared to speak. Then the superior turned to Anthony and bade him preach to the assembled friars whatever the Holy Spirit might inspire him to say. He was of the opinion that Anthony was without theological training and at most had learned only those things he would need to exercise his priesthood. Anthony, as far as he knew, spoke Latin rarely

26

and only when necessity required it. Though Anthony possessed so rich a knowledge that his memory served him like an open book and had all the requisites of a talented preacher, the other friars present also thought he was more fitted to clean the pots of the scullery than to explain the pages of Holy Writ.

Anthony resisted as long as he could. But since the audience seconded the request of his superior, he began at last to speak in a simple, humble way. But the longer he spoke, the more vivid and forcible became his words, until it seemed to the friars that the Holy Spirit himself was inspiring him to utter the words of his sermon. Astounded and fascinated, the friars listened attentively to his words, because he spoke to them so eloquently of the deep mysteries of faith and revealed a wealth of profound knowledge which they had never suspected in him. The thorough acquaintance with Holy Scripture and the great love of God and neighbor which were reflected in his words, no less than the enthusiasm with which he spoke, caused them to listen with breathless attention. From that time his confreres held him in high esteem, not only because of his humility, but also for his extraordinary eloquence and erudition.

The power of fire overcomes all things and is not itself subdued; it imparts its action to the things it encompasses, renews everything that comes near it, and does not decrease as it spreads itself. So too does the Holy Spirit pervade all things by his power, for he is ineffable in his might. When he enters a soul, he fills it with his fire, and lets it enkindle others. All things that draw near him feel his renewing warmth. He leads all hearts upward to heaven.

Apostle of the Pulpit and the School

A city set on a mountain, our Lord says, cannot be

27

hidden. Neither do men put a lamp under the measure, but upon the lamp-stand, that it may give light to all in the house. After the sermon at Forlì Anthony could no longer be hidden, for the Lord had set him like a lamp on the lamp-stand, that his light might shine on the whole house of the Church. For him, it meant the end of his contemplative life at Montepaolo and the beginning of a new apostolate.

It is likely that he received the commission to preach from his superior at the Chapter of Michaelmas, in accordance with the ordinance introduced by St. Francis: "Each year on the Feast of St. Michael the Archangel each minister can convene with his friars, wherever it may please him, to treat of the things that belong to God." Such an appointment would empower him to preach in the whole Franciscan Province of Romagna, which in those days embraced besides Romagna itself, Lombardy, Emilia, and the districts of Rimini, Venice, and Friuli. Anthony now exchanged his beloved solitude for the busy and distracting life of a wandering preacher, but he did it without reluctance. He had loved the quiet of Montepaolo because of the progress he had made there in the religious life, but he treasured even more the life of an apostle: *The world is like a field, and to bear fruit there is as difficult as it is praiseworthy. The hermits bloom in solitary places and shun the company of men. The monks blossom in a garden enclosed and hide themselves from the eyes of men. How much more glorious is it if a Christian brings forth fruit in an open field, the world, for all too easily the twin sprouts of grace; the spirit of a life of virtue and the fragrance of a good name, wither there and die. Therefore did Christ glory in being a flower in the field, since he said of himself: I am the flower of the field.*

Thus did Anthony, in obedience to his superiors, joyfully give himself to the apostolate of preaching. Because he was filled with the wisdom of God and guided in all things by the spirit of the Poverello of Assisi, the seeds of his preaching fell upon good ground. He always adapted himself to the circumstances and needs of his hearers. In Umbria, where the faith flourished, Francis and his sons had sought primarily to preach by their good example and to follow up this silent apostolate with only a brief word of admonition or exhortation, as Francis called it. But in the regions of upper Italy circumstances were quite otherwise, for here the preacher had to speak to heretics or to men who were infected with error or menaced by false doctrine. Besides the Cathari or Albigensians, whose center of influence was really in southern France, there were especially the Humiliati, who were allied with the Waldensians. They lived in strict poverty and maintained themselves by some manual trade; they were scandalized by the rich possessions of the Church and the worldly ways of many priests, and demanded that these priests return to the simplicity of the Apostles. As a result, they shunned the hierarchy and clergy and the sacraments of the Church, substituting a clergy and ritual of their own choosing. Because they and not the priests of the Church followed the poverty of the Apostles, they claimed for themselves the right to carry out Christ's command to the Apostles to announce his gospel message to all the world. Sometimes they maintained that it was not the sacrament of Holy Orders which bestowed the power to preach and administer the sacraments but purely and simply the imitation of the example of the Apostles. Hence, though they were only lay people, they considered themselves to be better qualified for the sacred ministry than were the priests of the Church. Despite their constant conflict with the Church, they were held in high esteem by the people because of their simple and exemplary life and thus were able to increase their membership steadily.

Anthony was convinced that it was not enough merely to preach the right doctrine in order to win men's minds and hearts, but that the preacher must confirm his words by a right and holy life: *The preacher must by word and example be a sun to those to whom he preaches. You are, says the Lord, the light of the world. The sun is the source of light and of warmth: a symbol of our life and our teaching—for like two streams these must overflow from us to men: our life must warm the hearts of men, while our teaching enlightens them.*

The clergy of his day were indeed, Anthony says, the cause of the prevailing evils, since they had failed in two ways: *Because in our times the priests of the Church do not possess the light of knowledge, while their life is lacking in true virtue, the wolf, that is the Devil, scatters the sheep, and the thief, that is the heretic, snatches them away.* How different was Anthony! What he preached he had made his own in prayer and frequent meditation. God was the ultimate source of his deep and rich learning, and what his tongue proclaimed came forth from his intimate converse with God. Later the Church could well apply to him the words of Holy Writ: "Because I prayed, prudence was given me; and because I pleaded, the spirit of Wisdom came to me." What he demanded of others he first cultivated in himself by strict self-discipline, penance, and a wrestling with God in prayer, as St. Francis required of his preachers. This was, he knew, a sad time in the life of the Church: had she not been forced, because of the laxity of her children, to decree at the Fourth Council of the Lateran (1215) that all must go to confession once a year and receive the Eucharist during the Paschal season? To him, then, the commission to preach was like the summons God had given of old to the prophet Isaias: "Cry, cease not, lift up your voice like a trumpet, and show my people their wicked doings, and the house of Jacob their sins." To him, the command of the superiors was the command of God himself, and like the Apostles he went forth and preached everywhere, in all the towns and villages of upper Italy, to announce to them the truths of Christ's Church and to do battle with the forces of heresy and error. The reason why his apostolate of the word had great success in those perilous regions and caused his hearers to admire him greatly, lay in the fact that Anthony himself was the best example and personification of what he preached. In his disputations he also showed that he surpassed the heretics in knowledge, and, as a true son and follower of the Poverello of Assisi, he lived in much greater poverty than they. By such spiritual means Anthony was able gradually but steadily to break the influence of the forces of error.

In this spiritual crisis Anthony knew no better means of saving souls, *no other remedy than the confession of sins, since after the shipwreck of sin the sacrament of penance is truly the second plant of salvation.* His hearers could not help admiring him when they perceived how ably he uncovered the causes and occasions of sins and exhorted them to a better way of life as Christians, Through his sermons, so the old biographers tell us, he showed men of all ranks and callings and ages the true way of salvation. He knew no respect of persons nor showed any partiality toward any of his listeners. And yet he knew how to adapt his words to his audience, so that all would draw profit from them. Those who were in error were brought back to the truth; those living in sin were made to feel sorrow and to desire to be reconciled with God; those who were leading a virtuous life felt themselves spurred on to greater zeal. Men said that he came to them like another Elias, consumed with zeal for God; and he appeared like a burning fire to the men of his day, stirring up by ardent words the lukewarm, drowsy, cold, and deluded hearts of his hearers, and enkindling in them the love of God. It was always his aim, whether preaching or counselling or hearing confessions, to reconcile men with God through the sacrament of penance

31

and to renew in their souls the divine life of grace. *We call confession the house of God because it bestows forgiveness on the sinner; it reconciles him to God as the prodigal son was reconciled to his father, when he was received by him into his house. Confession is also called the gate of heaven. Truly it is the gate of heaven, the gate of paradise, since it leads the penitent to God, that he may kneel and kiss the foot of the all-merciful Lord, then be lifted up to kiss the hand of our gracious God, and finally embraced by our loving Father and received to the kiss of his mouth.*

Another task was confided to Anthony when St. Francis commissioned him to teach theology to his fellow friars: "To Brother Anthony, my bishop, I Brother Francis send greetings. It pleases me that you should teach the friars sacred theology, provided that in such studies they do not destroy the spirit of holy prayer and devotedness, as is contained in the rule. Farewell." This letter was to mark a turning point in the history of the Franciscan brotherhood.

Just as Francis had never received the priesthood but wished to remain a deacon until his death, so his order at first counted few priests. There were, however, among the friars many learned brothers who had previously gone to schools or universities and who now wished to see studies fostered and regulated in the order. True, Francis had expressly bade his brothers to "honor and reverence all theologians and those who impart the most holy words of God, as those who minister to us spirit and life"; yet, in the beginning, he was opposed to the study of theology in his order because he feared that the friars might lose their simplicity and humility, and also because he did not consider study as necessary for their calling: "My friars who are led by such a spirit of curiosity will find their hands empty on the day of judgment," he would say. "Let them rather grow strong in virtue, that when the time of trouble comes they may have the Lord nigh unto them. For such tribulation will indeed come, when books will be tossed into corners and niches as being of no use whatever." "He did not say this," his biographer, Thomas of Celano, remarks "because the study of Scripture displeased him, but to keep his sons from a needless desire of learning and because he wished them to be truly good through love and not half-wise out of mere curiosity."

As long as the friars remained only among the faithful of Umbria, they had no great need at all for learning, since their sermons were simple and brief exhortations. The situation was quite different, however, when in upper Italy they came face to face with heretics or had to deal with people who were threatened by heresy. It was certainly not accidental that Anthony, the trained and well-grounded theologian, had such success in preaching to these people. His hearers expected the preacher not only to announce to them the teachings of the faith, but also to be more than a match for heretics in any disputation he might have with them. Thus the Friars Minor soon discovered that without theological training they had no way of getting at the Bible-shouting heretics in their sermons and disputations. Convinced that a sound theological training was indispensable, they approached Anthony and begged him to undertake the task of teaching them. Anthony agreed, but like a true Franciscan declared he could fulfill their request only with the permission of St. Francis. It was then that Francis, in the letter quoted above, changed his earlier attitude toward the study of theology among the friars. The exemplary life of the first theologian in his order had made it easy for him to overcome his prejudice against the scientific study of the faith.

Anthony thus began to teach theology to his fellow friars and became the first lector in the order. He is considered the founder of the course of studies in the convent of Bologna, which soon became famous as a school and housed many diligent students. Anthony, who as a canon at Lisbon and Coimbra had been a deep student of St. Augustine as well as of Holy Scripture, now blended the teachings of this great doctor with the ideals of the Seraphic Francis, a characteristic which was later to be the characteristic mark of the whole Franciscan School. In those days the study of theology was called simply the "study of Sacred Scripture" because the truths of Christian faith and morals were expounded in connection with the text of the Sacred Books. Anthony, as we know, possessed a deep knowledge of the Bible; and he had so impressed the Scriptures on his memory that he could have restored it word for word if it had been lost. At the same time, he had an extensive knowledge of the Church Fathers and the holy doctors, though his philosophical and scientific knowledge was quite modest and reflected the deficiencies of his time. Because his instructions were directed entirely to the priestly work and activity of his confreres, all his knowledge (as St. Augustine would have wished it) was put to the service of sacred doctrine.

To develop the full richness of theology, Anthony did not limit himself to the natural or literal sense of the sacred texts, but introduced his hearers to the spiritual understanding of the Holy Books, that they might see the deeper meanings of God's word. Sometimes, with the help of the allegorical sense of the text he joined one truth of faith to another, to make one body of doctrine out of them; and by such spiritual understanding of Holy Writ, he showed what Christians were to believe. The so-called anagogical sense, which explains the text from the viewpoint of eternity and man's happiness with God, helped him to point out what the Christian was to hope for. Finally, Anthony revealed through the moral meaning of the Sacred Books what the Christian must do. Through this sense he could develop his ascetical-mystical theology and teach by word what he already taught in action. For this science he often called to his aid the western Fathers of the Church, Augustine, Gregory the Great, and Bernard of Clairvaux; but, in general, he took a rather reserved stand toward the teachings of pseudo-Dionysius the Areopagite. He showed himself a true disciple of the Seraphic Francis when with him he made interior love for the humanity of Christ and his Passion, and the practice of Franciscan poverty, recollection, solitude, and the other virtues the very center and heart of his teaching. Last but not least, he was able to draw on his own personal experiences in giving practical instructions on virtue and morality; for, from the very beginning of his life as a friar, he gave to all an example of the contemplative life, of deep humility, prompt and joyful obedience, zeal for souls, and all the virtues.

Sacred theology was to Anthony a rich treasure, and was to be preferred to all other knowledge because of its greater excellence. Adapting the words of the Psalmist, he wrote: *Sing to the Lord a new song. All worldly wisdom is an old song, the canticle of Babylon. Only theology is the new song, for it alone pleases God by its melody and brings new life to the soul.* While the heretics of his day usually accepted only the New Testament as the inspired Scriptures and rejected the revelation of the Old Law, Anthony saw Christ as the center of both parts of Scripture: *There is but one and the same God in the Old and in the New Testament, Jesus Christ the Son of God. Here you have a clear witness against the heretics, who teach that Moses received the Law from a God of darkness. The God of the Jews, who gave Moses the Law, is the Father of our Lord Jesus Christ.* Anthony is thoroughly Franciscan also when he declares that all theological learning should be a means of promoting, not one's own glory, but the salvation of men: *It alone makes men learned, for it alone gives that salutary knowledge which teaches us to love God, despise the world,*

35

and bring the flesh into subjection. For him, theology should never be studied merely to satisfy human curiosity: *Often there comes to us the temptation to ask questions about many things, and yet who is so wise that he can have an answer for everything? All such questions are temptations; hence there is no wiser solution than to disregard them. He who is a searcher of difficult things, says the Wise Man, shall be overwhelmed by their greatness. Let us praise God in simplicity!*

His superiors were soon to call Anthony to another field of labor, but first his unwearying round of preaching was to have another great triumph. In his desire to save those who had fallen into heresy or were attracted by it, he invaded the very stronghold of the heretics, the city of Rimini. When he saw how many had fallen into error, he soon called the inhabitants of the city together; and, deeply stirred by their foolish aberration, he began to speak to them of the true and pure Faith of Christ. Here his ability to carry on a disputation proved its worth, for he was able to unmask the fallacies of the heretics and to refute their false teachings. His powerful words and salutary teaching fell on good ground in the hearts of his hearers. Not a few of those who listened to his words were led by his preaching to renounce their false beliefs and to return to the Lord. Among them was a man by the name of Bonillo, who had held heretical ideas for some thirty years and had advanced to the so-called "class of the perfect." Through his servant Anthony, God gave this man the grace of recognizing the truth. Bonillo accepted the penance which Anthony laid upon him, and he remained faithful to the commandments of the Church till his death. Later on the success of this mission seemed so marvellous that some thought it should be attributed not only to the words of the Saint but to a miracle. According to one legend, Anthony at first preached to deaf ears; and so he went to the banks of the river and preached to the dumb fishes. Only after these had given Anthony their attention, did the heretics listen to his words.

THE HAMMER OF HERETICS IN FRANCE

A New Field of Labor

In those days France was harassed by the demon of heresy, who as St. Peter said, went about as a roaring lion, seeking whom he might devour. The sect of the Cathari, who were also called Albigensians (from the headquarters of their sect, the city of Albi), was stronger and more widespread here than in upper Italy. Since instruction, exhortation, and spiritual punishments had been ineffective, the secular arm had waged a bloody Crusade against them since 1209. After the sack of Béziers in that year, the war grew even more fierce as the heretics defended not only their beliefs but also their very political liberty against the centralizing tendencies of northern France. To this unhappy land Anthony was sent by his superiors in 1224, in the hope that after gaining renown and enjoying success as a preacher against heretics in Italy he might by similar peaceful means achieve a fresh victory for Christ the King in southern France. In this spiritual crusade he had as a predecessor no less a personage than St. Dominic.

It was no easy task that awaited Anthony in France, for it was to bring him suffering, anxiety, and trouble. Yet, like a true son of the Poor Man of Assisi, he reminded himself that like his Seraphic Father he must ever be merely a pilgrim and stranger upon earth, and could expect to have lasting peace only in his heavenly fatherland: *On their pilgrimage in this strange land Christians will suffer many trials and needs and tribulations, for they are as strangers and pilgrims. A stranger is one who has come from another land; a pilgrim, one who wanders far from his homeland. We are*

37

all strangers, because we have come from another land, from the joys of Paradise, into this land of exile and banishment; and pilgrims, because the anger of God has cast us out, and like beggars we wander far from our heavenly home. It was with such sentiments that Anthony received the command of his superiors and journeyed to France. His only armor against the onslaughts of heresy was his deep theological learning and above all his great love and his willingness to suffer that he might win over the hearts of those in error. Like Francis who had gone unarmed into the very camp of the Sultan, Anthony rejected the use of all force or arms to gain a victory over heresy.

The journey was a long and difficult one, made on foot in slow stages. It seems likely that it led Anthony through the city of Parma; for, the Franciscan friary there (now a prison) cherished an old tradition that Anthony sought hospitality with his fellow friars in that town while on the way to France.

After he left Parma and continued his journey to southern France, he may well have stopped also at Vercelli and visited the famous and learned Augustinian Canon Thomas Gallus, who a few years earlier had become the abbot of the newly erected Abbey of Sant' Andrea di Vercelli. Later accounts tell us that, together with his English confrere Adam Marsh, Anthony spent some five years at Vercelli as a pupil of this learned abbot. The historical truth is simply that Anthony was a friend of this abbot, and that through the latter, who had translated into Latin the writings of the so-called Dionysius the Areopagite and commented on them, he had made the acquaintance of this mystic of the Christian Orient. It was quite in keeping with their friendship, therefore, that Anthony, whose way to France led him close to Vercelli, should visit his old friend and honored master.

The friendship of Anthony with the learned abbot is

commemorated in the frescoes which surround the tomb of Thomas Gallus. Among the persons pictured is to be found the youthful figure of Anthony. It was a friendship that survived beyond the grave; for, soon after his death Anthony appeared to the abbot in a dream and said to him, alluding to his own death: "I have left my ass in Padua, and I am now returning to my home." Had not Francis too been accustomed to speak of the body as Brother Ass? On the other hand, Thomas Gallus left his friend a lasting memorial in his writings. In his commentary on Dionysius, he cited Anthony as a perfect example of how a loving heart can penetrate much farther than cold rational knowledge into the mysteries of God: "Often," he wrote, "love can enter where mere natural knowledge is excluded. We read of some holy bishops that they were but poorly versed in the natural sciences, and yet they had the gift of readily understanding mystical theology. Having left all natural knowledge behind, their purified souls ascended as it were to the very heavens, even to the most Blessed Trinity. This very thing I myself, as a close friend, have been able to observe in the holy Brother Anthony of the Friars Minor. Though he was not well-read in the natural sciences, he had a pure spirit and a burning heart and was a man on fire for God. All this enabled him easily to understand all the riches and depths of mystical theology with all his heart. Therefore I may well apply to him the words which Sacred Scripture says of John the Baptist: He was a lamp, burning and shining. Because his heart was burning with love for God, he was a shining example also to men."

Souls dedicated to God are like the birds of the air, for they are lifted up on high by the wings of virtue and behold the King in his glory. Not in body, but in spirit, they are carried upward to the third heaven and see with the clear eyes of the spirit the majesty of the triune God, perceiving with the ears of their heart things which they cannot ex-

39

*press in words or grasp with their minds. The taste of God
in contemplation is more precious than everything else; for,
no matter what a man might wish for, it is nothing when
compared to this. For, when the spirit of a man stands
before God and sees his happiness and tastes his delights,
then in truth has he attained to paradise.*

*All the graces of God in this present life are only a little
drop in comparison with his eternal recompense.*

After his short visit with Abbot Thomas at Vercelli,
Anthony continued his long, tiresome journey to France.
Nothing has come down to us in regard to the exact route he
followed; yet, since he was once offered hospitality by a
noble lady of Annecy, it may well be that his way over the
Alps had brought him to that city. This great lady, who was
carrying a child beneath her heart, recommended herself
and the infant to the prayers of the Saint. Anthony immediately betook himself to prayer; and when he returned,
he said to her: "Be of good cheer and glad heart! For the
Lord will give you a son, who some day will be a great son of
the Church, a Friar Minor, and a martyr who will encourage
many others to suffer martyrdom too!" And so it turned out.
The good woman gave birth to a son, who was given the
name of Philip at his baptism. Later on, he became a
Franciscan and went as a missionary to the Holy Land.
Years later, in 1288, Azotus (Esdud), one of the last strong-
holds of the Christians acquired during the Crusades, with
some two thousand Christian inhabitants, was betrayed
into the hands of the Saracens. The Sultan imprisoned all
the Christians and condemned them to death unless they
abjured their Faith. Then Philip asked that he be the last to
be executed, for he wished to exhort the others to stand fast
and to be true to the Faith. As one after the other was led to
execution, Philip bravely encouraged each one to trust in
God and die for him. Then as the account of his glorious

martyrdom tells us, he himself became the last victim of the wrath of the Saracens.

Slavery in freedom and freedom in slavery! It is not fear that makes one a slave, nor love that makes him free. Rather, it is fear that makes him free, and love that makes him a slave. There is no law laid down for the just man, for he is a law unto himself: for he has charity, whereby he lives according to his conscience, and therefore he goes where he wills and does whatever he wishes. I am your servant, says the prophet, and the son of your handmaid. Note the words: servant and son; because he is a servant, he is also a son. O sweet fear, which makes a son of the servant! O merciful and true love, which makes a servant of the son! If you, O man, would enjoy freedom, then put your neck in the yoke and your feet in the fetters of love. There is no greater joy than this freedom. If a man bends not his stiff neck under the yoke of humility and puts not the feet of his sensual desires in the chains of penance, he cannot attain to this freedom. Only when he does this can he say in truth: I am your servant.

Follow after Christ and carry your cross for your salvation, as Christ carried his Cross for your salvation!

"Let none who follow this manner of life be called 'prior,'" St. Francis ordered in his rule, "but let all be called by the common name of 'Friars Minor.' And let them wash one another's feet!" An instance of such brotherly love Anthony was to experience when in the same year he arrived at the friary of Arles. Here the minister provincial, John Bonelli of Florence, had called his friars together for the chapter of Michaelmas, 1224. Since Anthony was a famous preacher and had come to France at the bidding of his superiors, the friars requested him to speak to them in the chapter. As he preached with great fervor and devotion on the title of the Cross, "Jesus of Nazareth, King of the Jews," Brother Monaldus, the companion of the minister

41

provincial, was looking towards the entrance of the house in which the friars were assembled. There he saw with his bodily eyes (as Celano relates) the blessed Francis, lifted up in the air, with hands extended like a cross in blessing upon the friars. At the same time all were filled with the consolation of the Holy Spirit, and the great joy which they experienced readily led them to believe what they heard of the appearance and presence of their glorious Father Francis.

In a sermon on the Cross of Christ St. Anthony says the following: *The Lord said to Moses: Make a brazen serpent and mount it on a pole, and if anyone who has been bitten looks at it, he will recover. The brazen serpent is an image of Christ the God-man. The bronze, which is not consumed by the ravages of time, stands for his divinity, the serpent for his humanity, which was raised up on the pole of the Cross as a sign of our salvation. Let us lift up our eyes, therefore, and look upon Jesus the author of our salvation! Let us meditate on how our Lord is suspended on the Cross and fixed to it with nails! But alas, as Moses cried also: Your life shall be as it were hanging before you, and you shall not be sure of your existence. And yet what does man prize more than his life? The life of the body is the soul, the Life of the soul is Christ. Behold then how the Life of your soul is hanging here! Why do you feel no sorrow, no compassion? If he is your Life, nay, because he is your Life, how can you keep yourself back from him? Must you not be ready with Peter and Thomas to go to prison, and to suffer death together with him? He hangs before you that he may arouse you to compassion for him. He says to you: All you who pass by the way, attend, and see if there be any sorrow like to my sorrow! Truly, no sorrow is like to his sorrow! For those whom he redeemed by so much suffering, he loses so quickly again. His Passion was indeed powerful enough to redeem all men; and yet see how almost all*

hasten to their damnation! Is there for him a greater
sorrow than this? Yet almost no one seems to care or think
of this. Must we not then fear that what God said of old: I
regret that I made them, he may now repeat in a new form:
I regret that I have redeemed them? . . . Again, your Life
hangs before you, that in it as in a mirror you may behold
yourself. In it you can know how mortal were your wounds,
which only the medicine of the Blood of the Son of God can
heal! If once more you look well into it, you can see your
true dignity and worth, since such an inestimable price
was paid for you. Nowhere can a man more clearly grasp
his dignity than in the mirror of the Cross. In it, you see
how you must bend your pride, and mortify the con-
cupiscence of your flesh, pray to the Father for those who
persecute you, and commend your spirit into his hands. . . .
The Cross may be called the wood of shame, for it is
written: Cursed is everyone who hangs on a tree! On it was
Christ the Wisdom of God the Father condemned and de-
rided: Ha, you who destroy the temple of God, and in three
days build it up again, save yourself! If he is the King of
Israel, let him come down now from the Cross. Yet, on the
Cross and through it, he has saved the world, which once
had been wiped out by the waters of the flood.

The Lord says: I thirst for the salvation of man. To what
did he hasten? To the Cross. Do you hasten after him, and
carry your cross for your own salvation, as he carried his
cross for your redemption! Whoever will follow me, he
says, let him deny himself by renouncing his own will, and
daily carry his cross by mortifying his body, and follow
after me. Thus follow me!

In the Camp of the Orthodox

From Arles Anthony went on toward Montpellier,
traveling in the manner in which St. Francis had exhorted

his friars to go from place to place: "When the friars go through the world, they should take nothing with them along the way, neither purse, nor wallet, nor bread, nor money, nor staff. And whatever house they shall enter, let them first say: Peace to this house! And they should remain in the same house, and eat and drink what the people have." Francis wished that in this way the friars should be a silent sermon to men.

In the crusade against heresy, which was still being waged, Montpellier was the central camp of the orthodox Christians. Here the Dominicans also prepared themselves for their future apostolate among the Albigensians, or Cathari, of the surrounding territory. Anthony had chosen this city as the starting-point of his apostolic work and preaching activity among these unbelievers, and as a training-post for his confreres who were to undertake the same work. This was in keeping with what Pope Honorius III had written to the University of Paris in 1217. "We earnestly beg your University, and by these letters request it, to send some among you to that place, that they may champion the cause of God, and, full of zeal, devote themselves to instruction, preaching, and exhortation." Anthony had a share in this concern of the pope. Besides his own zealous preaching activity, he also undertook to prepare his fellow friars in the new house of studies at Montpellier for their own apostolate by teaching them Sacred Scripture. Among other things, he began to explain the Psalms to them. Then one night a newly received novice decided to leave, and took with him the manuscript of the Psalms which contained also a marginal gloss Anthony had been using for his lectures. The Saint was naturally grieved at the loss of such an important book, and asked God to help him recover it. The novice, we are told, did not get very far; for he turned back when he arrived at the bridge near the city. Struck by remorse and contrition, he returned with the book to Anthony, confessed his fault, and asked to be allowed to re-enter the order once more. Later legends have added fantastic details to this incident: his remorse of conscience was turned into a terrifying appearance of the Devil who threatened the fleeing novice with a great sword and said to him: "Return to Anthony the servant of God and bring back the psalter to him, and rejoin the order. Otherwise, by God's command, I shall kill you and toss you into the river." The ex-novice hesitated and made no move to return, until he saw suddenly that the Devil was gradually becoming bigger and blacker and more horrible each moment. Finally, sheer fright drove him back to the friary.

This was a busy time for Anthony, since he combined such teaching with frequent preaching throughout the whole district. He visited all the cities and towns, to strengthen the faith of those Catholics who were still loyal, and to bring back to the fold those who had already wandered into error. Even today the sketches and outlines he made for his sermons give us a clear picture of how well he could adapt himself to simple men and speak to them in their own language.

Christ came forth from the bosom of the Father and came into the world to scatter his seed and to found his Church, that in her might be preserved that seed which does not corrupt but remains forever. Christ sowed three kinds of seed upon earth: his holy and praiseworthy life, the good tidings of the kingdom of heaven, and his miracles. See how rightly the word of God is compared to the seed! Just as the seed, so is the word of a sermon sown in the earth and then springs up and bears fruit. First, it pushes forth the blade, then the ear, and at last develops the ripe grains in the ear. When the word of God is sown in the heart of the sinner it too brings forth a blade, that is, contrition; this in turn produces the ear, of confession; and finally appears the ripe grain of satisfaction. Yet all our labors are worth nothing if God's help is not present to us. But what is begun with God's blessing soon goes speedily forward. And what grows so well remains in good condition. But what is good and firm establishes Christians in the love of God, and in the end crowns them with the reward of eternal life.

From Christ, as from the center, stream forth all graces to us who are in the circumference. When the soul lies before him like fertile land, it is a Garden of Eden in which bloom the rose of love, the violet of humility, and the lily of purity.

In the Stronghold of Unbelief

To remain at Montpellier was to wage a defensive battle only. The day came when Anthony was able to venture forth into the very heart of enemy territory, the city of Toulouse. As he went along the ancient road toward this capital of the Albigensians, or Cathari, he passed by the stubborn little town of Carcassonne, which lay on top of a mountain. Surrounded by ramparts and strong stone walls, it seemed to defy any assault. For Anthony this was a figure of the Church, *whose ancient enemy, the Devil, is constantly besieging her with the onslaughts of heresy and the attacks of false Christians. To her applies the word of the Lord: I have made you this day a fortified city, and a pillar of iron, and a wall of brass against all the land. A fortified city signifies the unity which establishes the Church in truth and protects her through its strength; the pillar of iron signifies the brotherly love which gives her a firm support; the wall of brass signifies her invincible patience and steadfastness in preaching the Gospel.*

He knew that as a son of the Poor Man of Assisi he was personally unassailable by the heretics: *As the bulwark protects the castle, so does poverty protect our life. Hence*

46

we have nothing to fear from the arrows of our ancient enemy.

At last he beheld from afar the old Cathedral of St. Sernin (Saturninus) with its stocky square tower, which was then the landmark of Toulouse. This city had been chosen by Count Raymond VI as the headquarters of his fight against the orthodox Christians and against the leader of the opposing forces, Simon of Montfort. It was really the stronghold of the Albigensians, though their spiritual center lay at Albi, some forty miles to the northeast.

Anthony had deliberately chosen this citadel of heresy as the scene of renewed activity on his part. Here he wished to school his fellow friars in the art of warfare against the heretics, while he himself preached in the city and its environs and entered into disputations with the heretics and their leaders.

As the Waldensians had originally been scandalized by the unworthy conduct of many of the clergy, so the Albigensians at first had merely inveighed against the unworthy conduct of priests of the Church. Later, however, they came into almost constant conflict with the Church and adopted certain false teachings of eastern heretics which had long since been condemned by the Church. Thus they believed that only the soul was created by God, while they regarded the body and everything material as the product of the Devil. In consequence, they denied the reality of Christ's human nature, the resurrection of the body, and the sacraments, since in all these the spiritual was bound up with the material. In their moral code, too, they strove to achieve a complete liberation of spirit from matter. In opposition to what they called the "carnal" Church they had set up for themselves a "spiritual" hierarchy; and for the sacraments they substituted purely spiritual means of salvation. Hence Catholics who were

47

tainted with such errors were usually very negligent in receiving the sacraments.

Besides giving his confreres a solid training in theology, Anthony once more turned the full force of his zeal against the false teachings of the Albigensians, and repeatedly he was able to refute publicly many of the leading heretics of Toulouse. He had such a command of the Bible and of the pertinent arguments of the Church Fathers that no heretic dared to challenge him or oppose him. Because of his restless zeal in the apostolate of preaching and his exceptional success in confuting every form of heresy he earned for himself the title of "Indefatigable Hammer of Heretics."

It is rather remarkable, perhaps, that in the sermons which he has left us Anthony but seldom takes issue with the heretics. To win back those who had gone astray, he preferred to present the grandeur of Christianity in a positive way. One exception may be found in his words on the Sacrament of the Eucharist; for they make some reference to the errors of the Albigensians, who denied the real human nature of Christ and the transubstantiation in the Sacrifice of the Mass: *Upon the altar there takes place the transubstantiation of the bread and wine into the Flesh and Blood of Jesus Christ. That Body which the Virgin begot, which hung upon the Cross and was placed in the sepulchre, which rose again the third day, and ascended to the right hand of the Father, this Body the Church today and everyday presents and distributes to her faithful. When the priest speaks the words: This is my Body, the essence of the bread is changed into the Body of Christ.*

His courageous defence of the real presence of Christ in the Eucharist, which convinced even the heretics, was probably the reason why later on the old legend of the miracle of the kneeling ass was introduced.

48

Chapel marking birthplace

Baptistery at which the Saint was christened

Bridge of the miracle of the psalter, Montpellier

Tomb of Saint Anthony

The Religious Renewal of France

Anthony did not remain very long in Toulouse. As soon as the confreres whom he had trained for the apostolate were capable of taking over his duties, obedience summoned him to a new task: he was chosen guardian of the convent at Le-Puy-en-Velay. In true Franciscan spirit, Anthony saw in this new office an opportunity to serve his fellow friars, as is indicated in the rule of the order: "The ministers and servants should recall the words of the Lord: I have come not to be served, but to serve, and they should remember that to them is committed the care of the souls of the friars. And should any of these be lost by their fault and bad example, they shall have to give an account of this on judgment day before the Lord Jesus Christ." The spirit which animated Anthony in his office can be described in his own words: *The good shepherd has eyes only for God and for the needs of his neighbor. Contemplation and compassion must truly be his guides. He who is strict with his subjects, keeps in the service of God all who follow the Lord, and saves them from the dangers of death. For this reason the superior descends and bends down to his fellow man. Only thus can he lift up his neighbor when the latter is prostrate. Happy the superior who through a good life leads a sinner to what is good!*

Once more, therefore, Anthony had to undertake a long journey, for the city of Le Puy lay some 175 miles northeast of Toulouse. Then already it was widely known for its pilgrimage shrine of the Black Madonna of Notre-Dame du Puy, in the cathedral church of the town.

From afar off he was able to see the "holy city of France" (as Le Puy was then called because of its sanctuaries) with its two rocky pinnacles which towered upwards into the sky. As he came near, he could see on top of the rocky eminence to the left the old church of St. Michel d'Aiguilhe, which is even now reached by a staircase of 265 steps. It seems to cry to the passers-by: Lift up your hearts, for the harmony of this church with its clock-tower and square nave and two apses well represents the duty of man here upon earth; namely, to use that which is natural as a stepping stone to the supernatural. This must have been the thought of the eleventh-century architect who chose the spot as a place to build a church which is a miracle of engineering.

On the right-hand slope of the other towering rock, called the Rocher de Corneille, in the middle of the older part of the city, is the ancient cathedral with its shrine of our Lady. This church, which is almost Byzantine in its gracefulness, is popularly called "The House of the Angels," because according to legend it was consecrated by angels. It enshrines the miraculous figure of the Black Madonna, made (we are told) by the Prophet Jeremias and given by the great Sultan of Babylon to St. Louis IX. Like the pilgrims who flocked here in great numbers, Anthony found not only a famous city like Toledo or Santiago de Compostela, to which the faithful came from all Christendom, but a center like Rome, London, or Byzantium, beautiful in its quiet splendor—the "holy city of France."

The work that awaited St. Anthony on his arrival at Le Puy was quite different from any he had done before. No longer did he have to face heretics and try to wean them from error by preaching to them and refuting their objections. The people of Le Puy-en-Velay were loyal to their Catholic Faith and were in no way endangered by heresy. Consequently, the mission of Anthony and his fellow friars was to show these loyal believers the way of salvation by their good example and their sermons from the pulpit. With Francis, Anthony was convinced that even the best sermon was without fruit if the preacher failed to make his own conduct agree with his words: *He alone preaches rightly who confirms by his actions what he announces by his lips.*

50

He who imparts the bread of God's word and does not fail to give witness to the truth through his deeds, will receive a blessing in this life and in the life to come. But alas, how many appear fair in their words, and yet are ugly lepers in their deeds! When merely the mouth of the preacher and not his life speaks, no fountain of water can come forth from the rocky ground. The face of the preacher is his way of acting, for in it is reflected his true countenance. This face must shine like the sun, that in our works all may see we have learned by faith. What we have grasped in our hearts as good, we must show outwardly also in our good deeds; and what we have tasted of God in meditation, must be reflected in our love for neighbor. So must our countenance shine as the sun.

Besides the friary in which Anthony was guardian, the whole town and countryside, the cathedral and the other churches, soon benefited by his apostolic labors. It may even be said that the memory of the sermons which he preached here, still survives. Though no particular sermon of that period has come down to us, we learn from Anthony himself what ideals he set before himself in his preaching: *The sermon must be true, not false, without frivolous, jesting, or high-sounding words, and it must call men to weep and do penance. Just as a thorn draws blood when it pierces the skin, and a nail that is driven through the hand will cause great suffering, so should the words of the wise man like a thorn pierce the heart of the sinner and draw forth the blood of his tears, and cause him to have sorrow over his past sins and fear of the punishment of hell. The sermon, moreover, must be sincere, which means that the preacher may not deny by his actions what he says in words, for the whole force of his eloquence is lost when his word is not helped by his deed. Lastly, it must direct its hearers to correction in such a way that, having heard the sermon, they will change their lives for the better.*

51

Later on, the sojourn of Anthony in this friary was commemorated in the martyrology in these words: "At Le Puy-en-Velay the memory of Blessed Anthony of the Order of Friars Minor. He led a most holy life, was famous for miracles, and here won great veneration." This statement, which we might well expect, goes on to describe his sojourn in Le Puy as follows: "He guided the friars with great prudence and kindness, and by his indefatigable preaching and his heroic example led men to a truly Christian life."

In the late spring of 1225 we find Anthony in Bourges, the capital of what was then the duchy of Berry in central France. Situated on a hill, this city seems to lord it over the whole countryside, yet it is itself dominated by the great cathedral of Saint-Etienne, which in St. Anthony's day was still in the process of construction. But even the unfinished edifice with its ninth-century crypt clearly told the visitor that Bourges was the see of one of the first archbishops of France, and that it was to become a fitting cathedral for the Primate of Aquitaine.

In this cathedral Simon de Sully, Archbishop of Bourges, had summoned a national council for the thirtieth of November, 1225, at which especially two pressing questions were to be considered: the fight against heresy, and the pacification of the unruly and rebellious populace of southern France. These matters were of such importance that the pope himself had sent his legates to the council. By now Anthony had acquired such a great reputation as a preacher at Le Puy that the archbishop made him one of his counselors, and commissioned him to preach to the council. During this sermon, Anthony, inspired by God, suddenly turned to the Archbishop with the words: "And now I have something to say to you who wear the mitre!" Then, moved by zeal for the things of God, he reproached the archbishop because of certain faults which burdened his conscience, and so ably and convincingly showed from Sacred

52

Scripture how evil they were that the great churchman broke into tears of sorrow. After the sermon the archbishop took the courageous preacher aside, revealed to him the wounds of his soul, and from then on became more zealous than before in the fulfillment of his duties as a prelate. This esteemed churchman, who was really among the best in France and highly regarded by both King St. Louis IX and Pope Honorius III, certainly revealed the greatness of his soul by his humility. Evidently, in his heart he knew Anthony was right in the belief that in such a crucial hour for the church of France any taint on the good name of the bishops and clergy could very well expose the faithful to the danger of heresy. On one occasion St. Anthony said: *God has set his priests as watchmen on the walls of Jerusalem. But because they are lax in their duties, the faithful fall into the snares of Satan. But happy the superior who through his good example leads the sinner to what is good.* Anthony goes on to explain what he means in words that are unusually courageous even for him; for he says of the failings of the clergy: *Wicked shepherds and priests of the Church form a group of people who curse their father and bless not their mother. They curse God their Father through their sinful life and neglect of their office, since his name is blasphemed on their account. They bless not their Mother the Church; instead, by their evil deeds they destroy in the Church the very faith they should preach by word and example.*

A still richer field of activity was allotted to Anthony from the year 1226 till Pentecost of 1227, in the district of Limoges, when he served as custos, that is, superior over several friaries. Limoges, which was already an important city and bishopric in the Middle Ages, really grew out of two adjacent castles. One castle included the abbey church of Saint-Martial which was built over the grave of the first apostle of the faith in that city and dedicated to him. It was believed that St. Martial was one of the seventy-two disciples of Christ, and was sent by St. Peter himself to evangelize this region. The other castle was connected with the cathedral of Saint-Etienne and was likewise well fortified. The Friars Minor had come to Limoges in 1223 and lived in a plain house which the Benedictines of Saint-Martial had given them. It was to be their home for some seventeen years.

When Anthony came to Limoges, he made his permanent residence with the friars and from there went forth to visit the houses subject to him. Hence he preached mostly in the churches of the town. We know for example that on Holy Thursday he preached from the pulpit of the church of Saint-Pierre du Queyroix (Saint Peter's of the Four Ways).

In a sermon written by St. Anthony for Holy Thursday, we read: *During the meal, Jesus took bread, blessed it and broke it as a sign that not without his free consent was his Body to be broken in death . . . The humanity of Christ is like the grape because it was crushed in the winepress of the Cross so that his Blood flowed forth over all the earth. This Blood the Lord gave today to the Apostles to drink: This is my Blood of the New Covenant, which shall be shed for many unto the forgiveness of sins. How great is the charity of the Beloved! How great the love of the Bridegroom for his Spouse the Church! His own Blood, which in the future he was to pour forth for her in the hands of the faithful, he himself offered to her today with his most holy hands.*

On him who receives the Lord worthily, he bestows his twofold anointing: He lessens temptations and he incites devotion. Because he makes the bitter sweet and nourishes the devotion of our heart, he is truly called the land flowing with milk and honey. Unhappy the man who enters this Banquet without the wedding garment of charity or of penance, because he who receives unworthily receives in

54

*himself damnation. What fellowship has light with dark-
ness or the betrayer Judas with the Savior? The hand of
him who betrays me, says Christ, is with me on the table.*
Anthony must have preached often also in the great
cathedral. At times when he wished to speak to the people,
he found his audience so large that not even the largest
church in the city could hold the crowd. On such occasions
he was obliged to give his sermons out in the open in some
large square.

One day, for lack of a church that was large enough,
Anthony went with his hearers to a place in the city called
the Sandpit (Creux des Arenes), where there was plenty of
room and where the people could sit down to listen to his
words. They followed his discourse as though they were
spellbound; for, not even the approach of a bad storm could
distract their attention. Since these were Catholic people
who were untainted by heresy, the preacher Anthony could
follow to the letter the admonition of his order's rule, that
the preachers should speak to the people, "in words that are
brief, of vices and virtues, punishment and glory." Often
too he must have taken as theme a subject that lay close to
the heart of his Seraphic Father, holy poverty. For such a
sermon a favorite text would have been the words of our
Lord: "The foxes have dens, and the birds of the air have
nests; but the Son of Man has nowhere to lay his head."
*Whoever is so enslaved by greed that he refuses to abandon
his love for the world or to regard all his riches as ashes,
should consider how the Son of God was wrapped in
swaddling clothes and laid in a manger, how he had nowhere to lay his head, save the Cross, on which he bowed
his head and died!* Another favorite sermon text, often used
by Anthony was: "There is nothing more wicked than to
love money."

As always, Anthony showed a tender concern for those
who were afflicted or sorely tried. One such person was a

young man of Limoges called Peter, who was among those whom Anthony's sermons on the Franciscan life had inspired to enter the order. The young novice's peace of soul was soon disturbed by the temptation to put off the habit which he had received from Anthony himself. Being a watchful shepherd of his subjects, Anthony called the youth to his cell, opened his mouth with his hands, and breathed into it with the words: "Receive the Holy Spirit!" The temptation vanished at once, and for the rest of his life in the order the friar was spared further assaults of the Evil One, so that in him the words of the Saint were truly fulfilled: *When the Holy Spirit becomes the Spouse of a soul, he clothes it with power from on high. From on high he gives strength to the weary, fortitude and power to the weak: strength, that it may rise up, fortitude that it may not fail in temptation, power that it may persevere unto the end.*

On All Souls' Day in 1226 Anthony preached in the courtyard of the church of Saint-Paul and took as his theme the words of Holy Writ: "In the evening weeping shall be our guest, but with the morning, rejoicing." In the sermon notes which Anthony has left us, he says: *There is a three-fold evening and morning, and in each of them there is weeping and rejoicing. The fall of Adam was the first evening of weeping, since he was cast out of Paradise and deserved to hear the words: In the sweat of your brow you shall eat your bread. The first morning was the Birth of Christ, in which there was rejoicing, according to the words of the angel: I bring you news of great joy.—The second evening of sorrow was the Death of Christ, according to his words in St. Luke: Daughters of Jerusalem, do not weep for me, but weep for yourselves and for your children. The second morning of rejoicing was his Resurrection, for St. John says: The disciples rejoiced at the sight of the Lord.—The third evening of sorrow is the death*

56

of every man, for we read: Sara died in Cariath-arbe, and Abraham began to mourn for Sara and weep over her. The third morning will come for the saints in the universal resurrection, for then, as Isaias says, everlasting joy shall be upon their heads.

As custos Anthony was also required to visit the friaries subject to him. The rule of the Order of Friars Minor contains this direction: "Those friars who are the ministers and servants of the others should visit their friars and duly admonish and correct them in humility and love. But they shall never command them to do anything that is against their conscience and our rule." The journeys of visitation also gave Anthony the opportunity to preach the truths of the Faith to the Catholic people of the towns and villages on the way and to exhort them to live as good Christians. On one such occasion he wished to preach in Saint-Junien, not far from Limoges, but found no church large enough to hold all who came to hear him. Here again he led the crowd to an open field, and there a temporary pulpit was set up for his use.

The praise of the most glorious Virgin is the sweet voice which delights the ears of the Spouse, Jesus Christ, the Son of that Virgin. For Wisdom, the Son of God, has built himself a house in the womb of the ever-blessed Virgin, and has set up this tabernacle on seven columns, the sevenfold gift of grace in Mary, Truly, blessed is the womb that bore you, O Son of God, Lord of the Angels, Creator of heaven and earth, Redeemer of the world!

O Cherubim and Seraphim, Angels and Archangels, cast down your gaze in awe and bend your head, and reverently venerate the temple of the Son of God, the shrine of the Holy Spirit, and exclaim: Blessed is the womb that bore you! O earthly sons of Adam, to whom this grace, this solitary boast is given! With faith and devotion, prostrate yourselves and honor the ivory throne of our true Solomon, the high and elevated throne of our Isaias, saying: Blessed is the womb that bore you!

On another tour of visitation Anthony fell sick, and stopped at the Benedictine abbey of Solignac in the diocese of Limoges, where the monks nursed him back to health. The monk assigned to care for him suffered from violent temptation of the flesh, and all his fasting, vigils, and prayers had not succeeded in freeing him from these assaults; for God had chosen Anthony to be his instrument to free the monk from his afflictions of soul.

After the monk had observed for some time the holy life of Anthony, he took courage one day and revealed to him in a sincere confession all his sins and the temptations that even then assailed him, and humbly asked for penance and absolution. Anthony drew him aside; and, taking off his own outer tunic, he bade the monk put it on. Hardly had the garment touched the body of the poor monk when all temptations suddenly ceased. Because he had graciously cared for the servant of God in his sickness, the latter in turn freed him from his torments of soul—and so perfectly, that he never again suffered from similar severe temptations.

The hand of the merciful God supports the just man, that he may not fall into sin; it strikes him that he may not become proud or presumptuous and thus flee from the grace of God our Father. For this reason the Apostle says: Lest the greatness of the revelations should puff me up, there was given me a thorn for the flesh, a messenger of Satan, to buffet me.

As the sail drives a ship, so let compassion lead you to care for the needs of your brother. But you, O heart of stone, you feel no compassion for your neighbor, for you say: Am I my brother's keeper? Know this, however, that if you were truly your brother's keeper, you would receive a great reward.

In his role as custos Anthony established a new foundation of his order in the city of Brive, which lies some sixty miles south of Limoges. This was a very plain and poor house, quite in keeping with the wish expressed by St. Francis shortly before his death: "Let the friars take care, that in no wise they receive churches, or poor dwellings, or aught else that may be built for them, unless these truly conform to the holy poverty which we have promised in the rule." The inhabitants of Brive were not very rich, nor were they really poor. Then as now they lived principally from the produce of their fields and farms, and often enough the results of their labors were spoiled by the caprice of the weather. The importance of this place is due especially to its advantageous location. From olden times an ancient highway, which runs through France from north to south along the River Correze, leads through Brive and passes over the river on one of the bridges of the city.

After he had founded this little friary, Anthony remained for some time in Brive, which today is still the center of devotion to him in France. He made himself a little hermit's cell in a nearby grotto, and spent many quiet hours in prayer, contemplation, and penance. Visitors are shown a fountain which Anthony made to catch the water that comes out of the rocks.

It is said sometimes that Anthony joined the Friars Minor not out of love for poverty, which was so dear to the Little Poor Man of Assisi, but from a desire for martyrdom. While there is a grain of truth in this, we may not over-emphasize it or conclude that for this reason Anthony loved and treasured poverty less than St. Francis, who had made it the special mark of his friars and in his rule indicated how greatly he prized it: "Like pilgrims and strangers in this world, who serve the Lord in poverty and lowliness, let them go begging for alms with complete hope in him. Nor should this make them feel ashamed, since for our sakes the Lord himself came into this world as a poor man.

Such indeed is the greatness of this perfect poverty, that it makes you, my dearest brothers, heirs and kings of the kingdom of heaven; and although you lack this world's goods as a consequence, you are made rich in virtues. Let this always be your portion here below, for it will bring you to the land of the living. Hold fast to it, beloved brothers, with all your soul, and desire never to have aught else under heaven, for the sake of our Lord Jesus Christ, whom you have chosen." In accordance with this ideal, the new house at Brive, for which Anthony had a great affection, was so poor that often the cook did not have anything to set before the friars at mealtime. Anthony would then go to a kind benefactress and ask her to give the brethren a few vegetables from her garden.

For Anthony this extreme poverty was not just an unavoidable feature of a new foundation, but rather a means of vanquishing earthly cares and a sure way of drawing closer to God. *When the spirit of a man has no rest because of his solicitude for earthly things, he cannot draw near to God. Hence if a religious wishes to be truly poor, he must do three things: first he must renounce all earthly possessions, and then give up even the desire to possess anything; and lastly he must bear in patience the hardships of poverty.*

Like Francis, Anthony regarded begging as the table which our loving Father in heaven has provided for all who are poor, whether by necessity or by choice. Francis had said of himself and his friars: "When the reward of work is not given us, then let us have recourse to the table of the Lord, and beg alms from door to door." Anthony, in turn, declares that *the table of the Lord is that poverty which Christ shared with his Apostles.*

His sojourn in the new friary at Brive thus reveals Anthony as a lover of the most perfect poverty and a true son of the Poverello. Living conditions in the friary, however, were not as exhausting as his prayers and penances in his quiet grotto. Brive also provided him with opportunities to preach; for soon he began to visit the churches of the town and the surrounding countryside, bringing God's truth and God's grace to all who desired it. His special love went out to those who had fallen into sin and had thus been ensnared by the Devil, the great enemy of God: *The Devil pursues the soul of the sinner like a man burning with jealousy and envy, and he makes use of all his cunning to prevent the sinner's return to God.* Anthony, therefore, always spoke to such men of the gravity and awful effects of sin and of the great misfortune of a sinner, who *in the night of his sins should consider what he has done, what he has lost, and in what he has become involved. He has incurred the death of his soul; he has lost the happiness of heaven; he has brought down on himself the punishment of hell.* There was hardly a sermon in which Anthony did not speak to sinners of *the mercy of God, which is greater than any wickedness in a sinner.*

Our knowledge of Anthony's stay in France comes from sources of a much later date, in which the great champion against heresy is so surrounded by incredible tales of miracles that the wonders of his preaching are quite forgotten. Yet these accounts are not completely without value for a proper appreciation of St. Anthony. Legends almost always have some historical fact as their starting-point, and so they do contain at least a grain of truth. In the stories about St. Anthony, for instance, we see that men turn to him in every need of body and soul and find in him a ready helper. Surely, the reason for this must be that, besides being an eloquent and successful preacher, Anthony must have distinguished himself by a deep compassion for suffering humanity.

These two characteristics of St. Anthony, his preaching and his compassion for others, artists have sought to represent when they place in his hand not only a book, as symbolizing his learning and preaching, but also a flame or burning heart, to show his love. These were the two ways in which he served the kingdom of God, and these two made him in truth the Servant of the Gospel and of the Church. Anthony himself has best characterized his own life in the prayer he said: *Let me live and die in the faith of your Apostles and of your holy Catholic Church.*

He was in truth, as Thomas Gallus said of him, a lamp, burning and shining!

THE NEW LIGHT OF ITALY

Contemplation and Apostolate

The house of the Franciscans at Monteluco near Spoleto makes the claim that both Francis and his true son St. Anthony loved its grottoes and solitary forests and sanctified them by their sojourn there. This is true. Both saints were deeply convinced that one must have the fire of God's love burning in one's own heart before one can enkindle it in the hearts of others. Time and again, therefore, after they had lived and worked for a long time among men, Francis and Anthony found themselves longing for solitude with God; and they would betake themselves to the hermitages of the order to live only for God in prayer, to do penance, and to work for their own sanctification.

Since Francis realized that the grace of the Holy Spirit is poured forth all the more abundantly upon a man the more he draws away from the bustle of the world, he sought poor abandoned churches or solitary spots that he might give himself to prayer; and he loved to pass the penitential season of Lent as a hermit in some abandoned wilderness. There, far from the haunts of men, he could give vent to his feelings. The woods and fields alone witnessed his sighs and cries over the sufferings of Christ; or, he gave himself to prayer, beseeching the eternal judge for mercy, petitioning the Father in heaven, or speaking to him as friend to Friend, and with a loud voice begging God to have mercy upon sinners. As a man of prayer and penance, Francis was indeed a pattern and model of contemplation for his sons.

Anthony shared fully in these thoughts and experiences of St. Francis. Once he complained: *Alas, how many disturbing thoughts go through our heart. As a result we lack the leisure to enjoy the bread of heavenly delights and to taste the joys of interior contemplation. For that reason the good Master invites us: Come apart from the restless throng into a desert place, into solitude of mind and body.* He himself, after he had worked hard and long for souls, would always feel an interior need for quiet, undisturbed prayer, and leisure to promote his own interior sanctification. He spoke from experience when he said: *When a man withdraws from the turbulence of the world and rests in quiet and solitude, tasting the bread of tears as he thinks over his sins, and relishing the delights of heaven, then does the Lord make himself known to him.*

All his life long, from the house of his parents to the cloister of the Augustinian Canons, and later to the Order of St. Francis, and again from his unsuccessful mission journey to Morocco to his happy days of contemplation on Montepaolo and then the wandering life of a preacher, Anthony had let himself be led by the Providence of God. So too, in a happy balance of the apostolate and the life of solitude, he surrendered himself after the example of the saints to the all-wise guidance of God. *The saints are like the stars. In his Providence Christ conceals them in a hidden place that they may not shine before others when they might wish to do so. Yet they are always ready to exchange the quiet of contemplation for the works of mercy as soon as they perceive in their heart the invitation of*

Christ. Anthony was actually experiencing the same indecision that had made Francis uncertain whether to adopt the contemplative or the active life, and that caused Francis to say: "What, my brothers, would you counsel? Should I give myself to prayer, or go about preaching? In prayer one obtains many graces, while in preaching one distributes to others what one has received from God. Prayer cleanses the heart of man and unites him with the one, true, and highest Good, and makes him strong in virtue. Preaching covers our feet with the dust of earth, brings many distractions, and easily weakens discipline. In prayer we speak to God and hear his voice, and we live a life like the angels and walk among them. In preaching we must go down among men and live with them and think, see, speak, and hear after the manner of men. Yet one thing seems to be of greater importance than all else, namely, that the only-begotten Son of God, who is the highest Wisdom, came down from the bosom of the Father for the salvation of souls to give the world an example and to announce to men the word of salvation. And because we must do all things according to the pattern we have in him, it seems more pleasing to God that we should sacrifice the quiet of prayer and take upon ourselves the toilsome apostolate of preaching."

In like manner, Anthony, who had dedicated his whole life to the service of the Gospel and the Church, treasured above all the peace of the contemplative life: *The active man traverses the earth to help his neighbor in need as the fish follows the paths of the sea. The contemplative is like the bird, for he is lifted by the wings of contemplation on high, to behold according to his capacity the King in all his beauty. If the spiritual man lays aside the cares and distractions of this life, if he enters into the house of his conscience and closes the door of his five senses, then he finds his peace in wisdom, because he gives himself to the contemplation of heavenly things and tastes the quiet of*

64

celestial delights. Like his Seraphic Father, Anthony gladly sought out the quiet grottoes in the woods of Monteluco, that he might be free to speak to God.

About Pentecost, 1227, Anthony was appointed provincial of upper Italy and returned to the scene of his former labors. The fame of his success as a preacher preceded him, and so this change opened up for him a large new field of apostolic work. Here he found a valuable helper and co-laborer in his confrere Luke Belludi, who like him was a celebrated and holy preacher and henceforth remained his constant companion and friend. (The honors bestowed upon him through the centuries were confirmed in 1927, when Pius XI declared him to be Blessed Luke Belludi.) When Anthony wished to spend some time in the stillness of Monteluco, he took the road from Spoleto, began to climb the mountain which lies south of the town and rises to the height of 2700 feet, and finally after an hour's walk reached the unassuming old chapel which the Benedictines had given the friars. The latter had built a poor dwelling out of mud and wattles near the chapel; and, in the great oak forest nearby, they had found a few caves on the side of the mountain. Here they could pray undisturbed, and as they gazed down upon the beauties of Umbria which lay at the foot of the mountain, they praised God as the mighty Creator of this wondrous world.

Anthony had a grotto assigned to him in this place. Even now we can read the inscription in it which tells us that he dwelt there: "This is the grotto in which St. Anthony did penance." Another inscription shows us that Anthony, who in Coimbra had once joined in the universal rejoicing at the triumph of the Cross over the Moors, put all his trust in the sign of our redemption: "Behold the Cross of the Lord! Begone, you evil powers! The Lion of the tribe of Juda, the Root of David, has conquered! Alleluia!" This prayer of the Church is now called the Brief or Blessing of St.

Anthony; for, he recommended it to his hearers, and advised them to use it, as he did himself: *Christ's love and Christ's sufferings drive out every kind of demon, because Christ has loved us with so great a love and has offered himself for us to God the Father as our ransom and a sacrifice unto an odor of sweetness. The fragrance of this evening sacrifice expels every sort of demon. When we are tempted by the Devil, who should pray with great fervor: In the Name of Jesus of Nazareth, who once commanded the sea and the wind, I command you, depart from me, you wicked spirit!*

During his work in northern Italy, probably around Easter, 1228, Anthony had to go to Rome for business of the order. Here he saw and spoke to Gregory IX, the former Cardinal Ugolino, faithful friend and adviser of St. Francis, who had been elected pope only during the previous year. The pope and many of the cardinals wished to hear a sermon from the famous preacher of the Franciscan Order. Because it was close to Easter, there were many pilgrims from distant lands in Rome. The pope, therefore, commanded Anthony to preach before the papal curia and the throngs of pilgrims.

Anthony had such a command of the Italian language, that it seemed hardly believable that he had lived elsewhere. This time, however, his words produced such an unusual impression that they captivated even those hearers who did not understand a word. In later times, it seemed quite incredible that his sermon should have such an effect, and men began to say instead that on this occasion the miracle of Pentecost was renewed; that the people in the audience asked one another in amazement: "Is not this man a Spaniard? How does it happen then that each of us hears him in the language in which we were born: Greeks and Latins, French and Germans, Slavs and English, Lombards and many others?"

Perhaps Anthony himself gives us the best explanation for the success of such a sermon when he attributes the results to the impressive appearance of the preacher and to his exemplary life which is a convincing sermon in itself. Anthony offers the following explanation in one of his Pentecost sermons: *He speaks in foreign tongues who is filled with the Holy Spirit. These foreign tongues are the testimony which we give for Christ, such as humility, poverty, patience, and obedience, by which we speak when others see these virtues in us. Our speech is alive when our works speak. I beseech you then, let words cease and let your deeds speak! Our life is so full of words but so empty of good works. And so the curse of the Lord comes upon us, for he cursed the fig tree on which he found only leaves and no fruit.*

Not only the pilgrims, but also the princes of the Church listened with rapt attention to his words. In this sermon Anthony manifested such a deep knowledge of the Bible that Pope Gregory IX later called him *Armarium divinae scripturae*, "the Armory of Holy Scripture."

Sometime after 1228 Anthony chose Padua as his place of residence, and since then his name has been inseparably linked with this city. Padua, which lies on the River Bachiglione, belonged at that time to the most important cities of Italy. It was a bishopric, and since 1222 possessed a university, which after Bologna enjoyed world fame for its faculty of Canon and Civil Law.

When Anthony came to Padua, the religious life of the city was at a very low ebb. The constant wars against the tyrant Ezzelino da Romano—head of the Ghibelline party, and a ruthless, brutal man—and against Padua's rival, the city of Verona, had undermined all public security. A radical reform was needed; for social conditions were such that in public and private life little remained of the genuine Christian spirit.

A short time after his first stay in Padua, Anthony withdrew into solitude for some time and wrote his Sunday Sermons, an extremely rich collection of material for all the Sundays of the church year. In it he assembled in orderly fashion an abundance of thought-provoking material taken from his own experience and activity as a preacher. It was to be a treasury, as it were, from which many, especially his confreres, could draw for their own use. At the end of this work, he writes: *Thus, my dearest brothers, I, the least of all of you, your brother and servant, have written this book to give joy to you, to edify the faithful, and to obtain the remission of my sins. I, therefore, beseech you and beg you most earnestly that when you read this work, you offer a remembrance of me, your brother, to God, the Son of God, who offered himself to God the Father on the gibbet of the Cross. I ask you also that, should you find anything in this work well said and properly arranged for your edification and consolation, give all praise, all glory, all honor, to the holy and blessed Son of God, Jesus Christ. Should you find anything poorly presented or expressed in a dry or inadequate way, impute it to my inability, my blindness, my stupidity. And whatever is found in this volume that should be deleted or corrected, I leave it to the prudent judgment of the learned men of the order to clarify and amend. Praise be to the Father invisible! Praise be to the Holy Spirit! Praise be to the Son, Jesus Christ, the King of heaven and earth. Amen. To the Alpha and Omega be glory, honor, and reverence! Praise and blessing to the Beginning without end. Amen.* In Padua itself this work no doubt proved to be most useful to him; for here too he undertook the theological training of his confreres.

The Franciscan friary at Padua was near the church of our Lady; it occupied the site where now stands the present Lombard-Gothic chapel in the Basilica of St. Anthony. Here Anthony soon resumed his apostolate of preaching.

His very first sermons won for him the affection of the people of Padua; and their attachment to him always brought him back to Padua, whenever he went elsewhere to preach or other duties called him away for a time. As confessor and shepherd of souls Anthony showed himself truly Christlike in the manner in which he dealt with the spiritual needs and problems of his penitents; and he was ready to help them also in their material needs. Thus we are told that one day a citizen of Padua by name of Peter brought his little daughter Paduana to the Saint. Although she was already four years of age, the little child was unable to walk and had to creep along on hands and knees. Her father told Anthony that she also suffered at times from epilepsy. Then the unhappy father asked the Saint to make the sign of the Cross over the girl. Anthony, seeing the faith of the father, gladly consented to his request. The father then set the child on her feet and coaxed her to make an attempt at walking, first with the help of a little footstool and then with the aid of a cane. After receiving the blessing of the Saint, the little girl made great progress in acquiring the use of her limbs, and finally was completey cured and no longer needed any support for walking. Later this incident did not quite satisfy the pious fancy of the Saint's devotees: the healing which followed upon the blessing of Anthony did not proceed fast enough. As the years went by after St. Anthony's death, the story became more detailed; the sickness of the child became worse; and the cure occurred sooner. In the end, the girl's first attempts at walking were quite forgotten, and the cure was represented as taking place immediately after the blessing of the Saint.

To satisfy the longing for solitude, Anthony suspended his activity in Padua and its environs for a while and betook himself to the famous mountain of La Verna, to spend some time in prayer and quiet. From Arezzo he walked through the valley of the Casentino to Bibbiena, some forty miles distant; and from there he made the long and steep climb to La Verna, a solitary peak, some 3700 feet high, with a commanding view of the whole surrounding countryside. The higher he went, the barer grew the fields and vineyards, the poorer the pastureland and the more rugged the hillsides. At long last, after a climb of some fourteen miles, he reached the wooded peak and could see, on the southwest corner, the little friary near the place where Francis had received the Stigmata of our Lord in mid-September 1224, around the feast of the Exaltation of the Cross.

"Two years before Francis yielded his soul to heaven," relates his first biographer, "he was dwelling in a hermitage called La Verna. There he saw in a vision a man standing above him, resembling a seraph, a man who had six wings and whose outstretched hands and joined feet were nailed to a cross. Two wings were lifted above his head, two were extended in flight, and the other two covered his whole body. And as the blessed servant of the Most High saw these things, he was filled with the greatest wonderment; but what this vision might mean, he did not know. Great joy filled his whole being; but even greater was his delight because of the kind, gracious look with which the Seraph, whose beauty was indescribable, regarded him. Yet at the same time his crucifixion and the bitterness of his Passion filled Francis with great dread. And so he stood up, being in a sense both sorrowful and glad as joy and sadness alternated within him. He was disturbed as he thought within himself what this vision might signify, and his spirit was troubled exceedingly as he tried to grasp its meaning. While as yet he understood nothing of it and his heart marveled at the novelty of the vision, there began to appear in his hands and feet the marks of the nails, in the selfsame way that he had seen them shortly before in the Man Crucified. His hands and feet appeared to be pierced in the middle with nails, so that the heads of the nails were visible on the inner part of the hands and the upper part of the feet, and their points could be seen on the other side. His right side too looked as though it had been pierced with a lance and then closed by a scar; and blood often flowed from the wound."

It was to this holy spot, then, that Anthony came, so that like his Seraphic Father he might dwell a while in the solitude of the mountain, alone with God.

This mountain had been given to Francis by Count Orlando da Chiusi in 1213; and Francis had immediately sent two friars to La Verna to build a few cells of mud and wattles in keeping with holy poverty. Later, during the years 1216-18, with the consent of St. Francis, Orlando had also built a modest chapel, dedicated to the Mother of God, "Mary of the Angels." The larger friary church and the chapel of the Stigmata date from later times. Francis loved this mountain with its silent woods and many caves and grottoes, because he could pray there undisturbed; and so he often visited it, especially during the many Lents he observed.

When Francis came to La Verna the first time, he stopped to rest beneath a great oak halfway up the hill. At once there flew to him from all sides a great flock of birds, singing and fluttering their wings. He regarded this as a sign that it pleased God, they should live on that solitary mountain. What Francis loved especially at La Verna was its many ravines and caves, in the darkness and solitude of which one could withdraw in holy retreat for days at a time, to be alone with God. One of these ravines, having ancient beech and oak trees, was the Sasso Spico, the ravine of the "Cleft Rock," which according to pious tradition had split open at the death of Christ and now provided a wondrous place for a life hidden in God. Not far from the Sasso Spico was a hidden grotto, a dark, cold cavern, where a dribble of water trickled from jagged rocks to the ground. In this

71

cavern is an oblong uneven slab of rock, which has long been called the "bed of St. Francis"; for, on it, so we are told, the Seraphic Saint took his repose when his tired body clamored for a slight rest.

Anthony shared his Father's love for these hidden caves, because there, far from human eyes, he could devote himself to prayer, and perform penances known only to God. He himself wrote: *The secret of the heart is like a veil that must hang between us and our neighbor, so that he cannot look behind that veil. It should be enough for him to see the lamps which we carry ready in our hands and which will give him light. For Jesus alone is our High-priest. All hearts are open to him, and he sees everything despite that curtain, for he searches the heart and its deepest thoughts.* Desiring to sanctify himself in secret, where only God could see him and he was hidden from the eyes of his confreres, Anthony withdrew from the little community of the hermitage on La Verna, and chose to live in complete silence and solitude in one of the grottoes of the mountain, thinking only of God and his soul. The little cave in which he dwelt as a hermit has been preserved and even today gives us some insight into the severity of his life of silence and penance. In memory of St. Anthony, it has been transformed into a little oratory; and pilgrims at La Verna are thus reminded of this little known side of his life.

The Messenger of Peace

"In every sermon," the first biographer of St. Francis tells us, "before he preached the word of God to those who had gathered, he wished them peace, saying: The Lord give you peace! Thus he greeted with great devotion not only the men and women who assembled to hear him, but also those he met along the way. As a result, many who had hated both peace and their own salvation came by God's grace to embrace peace with their whole heart, and became themselves sons of peace and zealous for eternal salvation." This message of peace belongs to the very calling of the Franciscans, which Francis described when he sent his brothers into distant lands and gave them the command: "Go, my beloved friars, two by two, to the corners of the world and announce to men the message of peace and penance unto the remission of sins."

Anthony stands out as a true Franciscan also in this respect. He too was a messenger of peace, especially in his sermons, in which he directed men to the way of peace and sought to keep them at peace with God. It was as a messenger of peace that he went to the general chapter of the order, called by the minister general, John Parenti, and held at the Porziuncola, the cradle of the order, May 25, 1230. Anthony took part in this meeting as the provincial of Romagna.

Because of his poor health and his apostolic labors, he begged to be relieved of this office at the chapter; and his request was granted.

At this chapter, an important one in the history of the order, certain doubts were raised concerning the binding force of certain points of the rule as well as the example and the Testament of the order's founder. In this matter two tendencies manifested themselves. On the one hand, the old "companions" of the Saint wished the order to return to the ideal life of the early years; for, they looked upon any development of the growing brotherhood into a strongly organized order as a betrayal of St. Francis. They were opposed by Brother Elias of Cortona and his followers who wanted to make the Franciscan Order as similar as possible to the older orders of the Church; and to achieve this end Elias was even ready to sacrifice essential features of the Franciscan ideal. On his part, Anthony sought to follow a middle course which would take into account the growth of the order and yet be completely faithful to the true aims of St. Francis. Since the two tendencies could not reach an agreement, the chapter appointed Anthony as the head of a delegation which was to consult Pope Gregory IX, the friend and counselor of their Seraphic Father. By reason of his long familiarity with Francis and the help and advice he had given him in the writing of the rule, Gregory was better fitted than anyone else to know the intentions of St. Francis and to solve the doubts of the friars. Thus it happened that Anthony came a second time to the papal court and once more made a deep impression on all by his erudition and holiness.

At this same chapter also the transfer of the bones of St. Francis to the new basilica took place. Soon after the Seraphic Patriarch had been canonized (July 16, 1228), Gregory IX laid the cornerstone for this church on the Colle d'Inferno (the Hill of Hell)—so called because it had been the place of execution for criminals. The building of the church had been entrusted to the influential and versatile Brother Elias, since the Pope had desired that a worthy church be erected over the tomb of the new Saint, a church which would make the place a "Hill of Paradise." By hard work, Brother Elias had actually succeeded, despite untold difficulties, in having the new friary and the lower church ready for the chapter (the upper church was finished only in 1253). It was an amazing accomplishment; for the nature of the terrain on this slope of Monte Subasio had required tremendous foundations for the church and friary. The strong and massive substructure of the friary and the grandiose outlines of the church give to the edifice the appearance of a mighty fortress which seems to lord it over the Umbrian plains.

Many have been scandalized on seeing the great basilica of the Saint who treasured poverty far more than any monument of architecture and art. Others have a more indulgent

74

view and have seen in this structure an expression of the high esteem in which St. Francis is held. In any case Anthony can be our guide; for, he points out that the true veneration of the saints is found primarily in the imitation of their virtues: *The holy life of the saints is like the sun shining upon the temple, for in its rays we can see the dust of our defects. We celebrate their feasts that we may find in their lives a model for our own.*

Francis died at the Porziuncola on Saturday evening, October 3, 1226. The next day, Sunday, his body was taken first to San Damiano, so that St. Clare and her sisters might see the Saint once more. Then it was carried into Assisi, to the church of San Giorgio, and there laid to rest. This little house of God, where Francis had learned his Latin as a boy and where he later preached his first sermon, was made a part of the Basilica of Santa Chiara (St. Clare), which was completed in 1260.

Because the lower church of San Francesco had been finished in time for the chapter, everyone expected that the body of St. Francis would be transferred from San Giorgio to the new church in a grand procession in which the legates of the pope and many friars would take part. With the cooperation of the civil authorities, however, Elias had already placed the relics of the Saint in a stone coffin somewhere under the lower church, because, so he said afterwards, he wished to forestall the possible attempt on the part of some to steal the precious treasure and carry it off to another place.

As one might expect, this autocratic act on the part of Elias evoked great disappointment and even exasperation on the part of the legates and the great crowd of friars who had gathered for the translation in the hopes of seeing the body of St. Francis once more. Some have said that Anthony was the spokesman of the embittered brethren and even claim he upbraided Elias. More recently, however, it has been proved that on this occasion Anthony again played the role of peacemaker.

Undoubtedly Elias meant well, but he was criticized by later sons of St. Francis inasmuch as the exact location of the tomb of their Father remained unknown. Finally, in 1818, with papal permission, excavations were made under the lower church; and after much labor the sarcophagus containing the relics of St. Francis was found. By further blasting and digging a crypt was then constructed beneath the lower church. Here, in an atmosphere of Franciscan poverty and simplicity, pilgrims now do what Anthony and his contemporaries could not do: they can kneel and venerate the remains of the Poverello, which now lie in the stone coffin over the altar; and they can pray to him from their hearts and implore him, as they honor his relics, that he might fill them with his spirit. Having returned to Padua and the Franciscan friary next to the Church of the Madonna, Anthony resumed the work he loved so much, that of preaching. The people of Padua, whom he had captivated in the very first sermon he addressed to them, clung to him with a singular attachment. In fact, his work as a preacher during this period became the high point of his whole apostolate.

At this time, early in 1231, the city was enjoying a little more peace than usual, and the people were in a better frame of mind to listen to his words than they had been during the troubled times which had gone before. The Lent of that year was to be a particularly fruitful time for Anthony. Men came in great numbers to his sermons, their hearts resembling parched fields that cried for rain. Despite the poor condition of his own health, Anthony was determined to fill their needs, and he preached to them daily during the whole Lenten season. The crowds were so great that no church could hold them. Hitherto Anthony had preached usually in the friary church or in other churches of the city or the vicinity; but now, his biographers tell us, he was forced to leave the churches, which were far too small for the throngs who came to listen, and, as he had done in France, went to the great piazzas of the city and sometimes even to the fields outside the town, in order to preach the word of God to the people.

Already on the previous evening the people gathered with torches at the place where the Saint was to preach the next morning. By about midnight the place was filled to capacity, old and young, men and women, all waiting patiently until the sermon would begin. Even soldiers and noble ladies were found in the audience. The bishop of Padua and his clergy gave a good example to all by attending frequently and listening carefully to the words of the preacher. At each sermon the audience seemed to grow larger, but it remained an orderly crowd. In fact, on some days there were upwards of thirty thousand present, yet there was no loud or boisterous demonstration and even the murmur of voices was hushed. Throughout the sermons, we are told, there was absolute quiet, and all listened with attentive hearts and minds to the words of help and consolation which the Saint addressed to them.

During the time of the sermon all the shops were closed; and even the merchants in the market place left their stands, not wishing to miss the sermon, and they did not return for business until the Saint had finished. Pious women who admired the preacher's holiness, sometimes secretly brought scissors with them, in the hope of cutting off a piece of his habit and bringing it home with them as a precious relic! To protect the Saint as he arrived in the morning or returned home in the evening, groups of young men of the town formed a kind of living wall around him and escorted him through the crowd.

These Lenten sermons became a religious revival not only for Padua but also for the surrounding district, since people came in great numbers to Padua from outlying villages and hamlets. To all, Anthony appeared as the herald of peace: his words achieved remarkable results. Quarrels were patched up, mortal enemies were reconciled, poor debtors were released from prison and given their freedom, restitution was made of ill-gotten goods. Bad women renounced their evil manner of life, thieves and malefactors became honest men once more, and the whole public life of the citizens and the state once more became Christian in character.

Anthony's main concern was to bring men back to peace with God. Hence, when the sermon was finished, he immediately began to hear confessions. Such a great crowd of the faithful, men and women, besieged the confessionals, that the friars and other priests of the city whom Anthony had called to his assistance, could hardly satisfy the demands made on them. Even with this help, Anthony, who began to hear confessions immediately after his Mass and sermon, often did not leave the confessional until evening. This meant that throughout the Lenten season he had to fast all day until nightfall. Among the penitents there were many who told their Father Confessor that a vision had brought them to his feet: at night in their dreams Anthony had appeared to them and counseled them to regain God's pardon and friendship by a good confession.

As a confessor St. Anthony was truly a channel of grace and blessing to many. The confessional, of course, is protected from human inquisitiveness by the veil of the seal. Nevertheless, pious tradition has given us a legend which illustrates the deep impression Anthony made on his penitents. A young man of Padua by the name of Leonard had confessed among other sins that he had kicked his mother so violently that she had fallen to the ground. By way of rebuke and warning, Anthony had quoted for the youth a proverb: "The foot that strikes father or mother

78

should be cut off forthwith." In his simplicity, the man went home immediately and hacked off his foot with an axe. The news of what he had done and the reason for it spread through the city like wild fire. When it reached the ears of Anthony, he came to the house, and after a devout prayer joined the severed limb to the leg by making the sign of the Cross over it. *A leper came to Jesus, fell down before him, and said: If you will it, you can make me clean. So should the sinner in confession kneel before the priest as the representative of Jesus Christ, who has given to him the power of binding and loosing. The sinner must have such faith in the dignity of this office that he too will say: Lord, if you will it, you can make me clean and absolve me from my sins. The leper was freed at once of his leprosy. God does this very thing each day in the soul of the sinner through his priest, for the priest also must do these same three things: he must stretch forth his hand, touch, and will. He stretches forth his hand when he prays to God for the sinner and is filled with compassion for him. He touches the sinner when he consoles him and promises forgiveness to him. He has the will to make him clean when he absolves him of his sin.*

During his stay in Padua, and more precisely from the last months of 1230 to the Lent of early 1231, Anthony in quiet retirement wrote his sermon-plans for the feasts of the saints throughout the liturgical year. This was done at the special request of Gregory IX, who had asked him to supplement his sermons for the Sundays of the church year with others for the principal feasts. When Lent came and he had to interrupt this task, Anthony had gotten as far as the sermon for the Commemoration of St. Paul. Little did he suspect that the work would never be finished because of his early death. There is a splendid manuscript copy of these sermons in the Treasury of the Basilica at Padua (*codex thesauri*). For a long time it was considered to be in the handwriting of the Saint himself; and hence it was looked upon as a very precious relic. However, it is now known to be merely a very old copy written by some other hand.

Another valuable document reveals Anthony's influence in the social sphere, and proves how great a messenger of peace he was. Even though it is not the original manuscript, it is a very old and official transcript from the laws and decrees of the city of Padua. From it we learn how Anthony applied the Gospel law of love to medieval life.

Up to that time, in keeping with the pagan-Roman concept of law which had been introduced some time earlier, a debtor or even a guarantor who could not pay might be imprisoned for his debts. A new law, which was passed at this time, was based on the milder principles of church law, according to which a debtor could be deprived of his possessions for the payment of his debts but not of his personal freedom.

Ancient statute from the year of the Lord 1231, the fifteenth day of March, under the Podesta Stefano Badoari. In the Name of the Father and of the Son and of the Holy Spirit. Amen. At the request of the venerable Friar (and holy confessor) Anthony of the Order of Friars Minor it was established and ordained that henceforth no one is to be held in prison for any pecuniary debt or debts, whether past, present or future, if he shall have agreed to relinquish his possessions; and this is to be understood both of debtors and of their guarantors. Furthermore, if any renunciation or cession or alienation shall have been fraudently made by the debtors or by the guarantors, this renunciation or cession shall not be valid nor have legal effect nor work to the prejudice of the creditors. And if such fraud cannot be proved to have taken place, the case shall rest with the judgment of the podesta. And this statute cannot be changed or limited or abolished hence-

forth and forever, whether by popular assembly or the city council or by any interpretation of jurists. And if this statute is not always found in the book of statutes and can be proved only through documents of this kind made by the keeper of the seal and notary De Zamboneto, the podesta shall nevertheless be bound to observe it, and he shall cause this decree to be entered in the statute-books according to the form of the documents, and the decree shall have the force of law.

This new law, as the document shows, was due to the influence of St. Anthony; and without doubt it was one of the results of his Lenten sermons of 1231. During this course of sermons, he used some very strong language to condemn usury, which had brought unhappiness to many families and often driven men to their death.

The cursed race of usurers grew great and strong upon earth. Their teeth are like the teeth of lions. Two things we note in a lion: his unbending neck and the reek of his teeth. So too the neck of the usurer is unbending, for he fears not God nor does he quail before man. His mouth is foul, for he puts nothing in his mouth save the dirt of money and the dung of his usury. His teeth are like those of a young lion, for he steals and crushes and swallows the goods of the poor, the widows, and the orphans. Anthony does not hesitate to call attachment to earthly goods a form of idolatry: *Those who love money and fickle honors, fall down before the Devil and adore him.* Time and again Anthony comes back to the folly of greedy practices. On one occasion he said: *The miser is not unlike the tumblebug which gathers dung and with much industry makes a ball out of it. Then an ass comes along, puts his hoof on the beetle and his ball, and annihilates both the bug and the product of his hard work. Thus do the miser and the usurer act. By long, hard labor they greedily collect filthy lucre; but in the end the Devil strangles them. And the result:*

their soul becomes the property of the Devil, their body that of the worms, and their riches go to their relatives. Earthly riches are like the reed: its roots are sunk in the swamp, and its exterior is fair to behold, but inside it is hollow. If a man leans on such a reed, it will snap off and pierce his soul, and his soul will be carried off to hell. After Anthony had thus gradually prepared men's hearts by his sermons, he could effectively suggest and demand a more lenient law for debtors. The preamble of the document mentioned indicates that Anthony was responsible for the change; it expressly states that the city of Padua issued the new decree at the request of Brother Anthony. The extant copy of the decree, however, was made after the canonization of St. Anthony.

It was but natural that in preaching about usury Anthony should make use of the words of Christ: "Where your treasure is, there is your heart also." Subsequently this circumstance served as the basis for another legend about St. Anthony, a story found also in lives of other saints. According to this account, Anthony had preached on the above words at the funeral of a usurer. The latter's relatives protested against the use of this text; but the Saint refused to retract what he had said. The relatives then opened the body of the usurer and found a stone substituted for his heart, but the man's heart they found in his treasure-chest! Thus did medieval piety express in a literal way what was meant in a figurative sense.

Anthony proved himself once more a messenger of peace when Count Riccardo da Santo Bonifacio, the head of the Guelph party, fell into the hands of his political enemy Ezzelino. He went straight to the camp of the tyrant at Verona, to obtain the liberation of the prisoner. This time, however, the Saint did not succeed. Though Ezzelino allowed Anthony to leave unmolested despite the reproaches he had hurled against the tyrant, the latter refused to set Count Riccardo free. "Even just requests," says a contemporary chronicler, "have no effect where love itself cannot succeed." A later legend has turned even this failure of the Saint into a miracle. Ezzelino is represented as saying: "When Anthony upbraided me, such a divine light flashed forth from his face that I was terrified and felt as though my soul was already slipping into hell. I fell down at the feet of Anthony, agreed to free the prisoner, and promised to amend my life." This legend, however, stands in direct opposition to what really happened. Anthony was so disappointed by the failure of his mission of peace, that after his return to Padua he decided to retire into solitude and devote himself to prayer and contemplation.

The sinner lives for the just man, that is, for the spiritual good of the pious; for the life of the sinner harasses the just man like red hot fire. God is said to harden the heart of a man when he withdraws or withholds his grace from him. Nothing worse can happen to a sinner than to be left in his wickedness of heart by the Lord and not to be brought to repentance by the fatherly chastisement inflicted on him by God.

Padua's Noblest Treasure

Anthony felt that his end was drawing near; but he carefully concealed this from his brethren, lest they worry about him. Toward the end of May he and a companion were standing one day on a hill near Padua. As he contemplated the city lying before him on the plain below, he was filled with great joy and said to his confrere that soon Padua would enjoy a great honor; but he did not explain in what this glory would consist.

The superhuman efforts of Anthony during the Lenten season had taken their toll. The Saint was now completely exhausted. Already at the beginning of Lent he had suffered one night from an attack of suffocation, but he had considered this to be an attempt of the Devil to thwart his plan of preaching daily to the people. Invoking the aid of the Blessed Mother of God, he had made the sign of the Cross, and felt himself immediately relieved; and when he opened his eyes, he saw the whole cell bathed in a heavenly light.

Now, however, his ebbing strength was becoming daily more evident. After the disappointment he had suffered in the meeting with Ezzelino, he ceased preaching and withdrew into solitude at Camposampiero. He wanted to prepare himself for Sister Death by prayer and contemplation. Not far from the Franciscan friary at Camposampiero a nobleman by the name of Tiso had a large field with many trees. Among these trees was a huge walnut, the trunk of which divided into six branches to form a kind of crown. When Anthony saw it, he desired to have a little cell built in the tree as a sort of hermitage. Tiso, who was a good friend and benefactor of the friars, immediately had a little hut built or woven into the branches of the tree; and close by he had two similar dwellings constructed for the Saint's companions.

In memory of St. Anthony's sojourn in this place the little church of Sant' Antonio di Noce (St. Anthony of the Tree) has been built where the walnut tree once stood. The cell of the Saint in a tree has often been pictured in Italian art, e.g., in the church of St. Anthony of the Tree (though there is no evidence that he preached from the tree).

In strict solitude, far from the crowds of Padua, Anthony now spent all his time in prayer, living only for God, and endeavoring by penitential tears to wash away all the stains of sin which, he believed, had sullied his soul while he was working among sinners. What he exhorted his hearers to do, he now did himself: *God permits his judgment to be exercised by the pious Christian; for the Christian judges himself and then God finds nothing in him that is worthy* *of blame. If we judge ourselves, says the Apostle, we shall not be judged.* O God, you have turned over your judgment to me, that I may pass judgment upon myself as you would and thus escape your judgment, for it is a fearful thing to fall into the hands of the living God.* On Friday, June 13, 1231, when the friary bell called him to the noonday meal in the refectory, Anthony left his cell in the tree and joined the little religious community. As he sat at table with his confreres, he suddenly experienced an attack of weakness, and had to be helped out of the refectory by the friars and put to bed in a nearby cell. Since he felt his end was near, he said to one of his confreres, Brother Roger: "If it seems good to you, Brother, I should like to return to Padua to the friary of Santa Maria, so as not to be a burden to the friars here." The friars did their best to dissuade him from leaving them, but in the end they yielded to his repeated request. Because his strength was so far gone that he could not walk, they put him in a wagon and set out for his beloved Padua. After they had gone a part of the way and were approaching the city, they met a friar who was coming to visit Anthony in his solitude. Seeing at once how weak Anthony was and how much the journey had sapped his strength, he begged the Saint to let his companions bring him for a while to the house of his confreres at Arcella. Here the friars had a little dwelling near the cloister of the Poor Clares, where they served as chaplains. He added very pointedly, since the friary of Padua was in the midst of a noisy city, Anthony would get no rest there and would not be able to escape the importunities of the people. Recognizing this as sound advice, Anthony yielded and permitted himself to be brought to Arcella.

Hardly had they arrived at this little friary, when Anthony suffered another attack which seemed to deprive him of his last remaining strength. After he had recovered a little, however, he confessed devoutly and received Viaticum.

Then he began to sing the well-known hymn to Mary, *O gloriosa virginum,* which in those days began with the words, *O gloriosa Domina,* and consisted of four stanzas: O glorious Lady, fairest Queen, exalted high in heav'n above! The great Creator, mighty Lord, by thee was nursed with mother's love. What sinful Eve had lost for us, by thy dear Son thou didst restore; the gate of heaven thou hast been made, that we may entrance find and weep no more. Through thee the Savior came to us, to be our guiding Light and King. To Christ, our Life, of Virgin born, ye ransomed peoples praises sing. O Mother dear of grace divine, God's mercy for us sinners plead, protect us from the enemy, in life's last hour to heaven lead.

After singing this hymn, Anthony kept his eyes steadfastly fixed toward heaven. When at last the friar who supported him asked what it was he gazed at so intently, he answered: "I see my Lord."

Since the friars saw that he was fast approaching his end, they prepared to administer the Last Anointing of the sick. When Anthony saw the holy oil being brought, he said to the friar who was preparing to anoint him: "It is not necessary that you administer this anointing to me, for I already have another unction within me. Yet it will be good for me, and it is well advised." After he received Extreme Unction, he prayed the Penitential Psalms together with the friars, holding his arms extended during the whole recitation. Then after perhaps a half hour had passed, his soul peacefully left his body and was received into the happiness of God's infinite love. After his death his body had the look of one sleeping, the hands became shining white, and his body remained without the usual rigidity which follows death. His demise was a happy return to God, such as he had often described to his hearers in his sermons: *When a little child comes running in tears to the arms of his mother, she comforts him and dries the tears.*

So too do the saints hasten from this world of sorrow to the arms of the Divine Majesty, and God wipes away all tears from every face. Behold, this is the end of tribulation, the goal of our way, the joy of those who seek, and the reward of those who find. The joy of everlasting fulfillment stills all our desires. So great is the beauty of God's majesty that it inflames those blessed spirits with a desire for it; and even as it incites their desires, it fulfills them and stirs up within them once more a renewed longing for God. Each saint in heaven rejoices over the glorification of the other, and his love overflows to him. Behold the pomegranate! All its seeds are enclosed within one skin, and yet each grain has its own cell. So shall there be in the glory of eternity only one house, one denarius, one and the same manner of living; and yet there shall be different cells for each; for, though eternity be the same, yet shall the place of each be different, since there is one glory of the sun, and another of the moon, and another of the stars. Despite this difference in splendor and glory, the same joy will fill all the blessed, for I shall rejoice over your well-being as though it were my own, and you will rejoice over mine as though it were yours. To use an example: see, we are standing together, and I have a rose in my hand. The rose is mine, and yet you no less than I rejoice in its beauty and its perfume. So shall it be in eternal life: my glory shall be your consolation and exultation, and yours shall be mine.

Anthony was only thirty-six years old when he died. Of these he had spent fifteen in his parents' home, two at the Abbey of São Vicente in Lisbon, nine in the cloister of Santa Cruz at Coimbra; and only the last ten years had he lived for God and souls as a member of the Order of St. Francis.

His departure, if we may apply to it what he himself said in his sermon at Limoges on All Souls' Day, was far less an evening of weeping and of death than a morning of rejoicing and of resurrection. The few confreres who at Arcella witnessed his happy passing to God, had considered it a forecast of his future glorification; and almost spontaneously their lips had formed the prayer: "You were truly a holy servant of the Most High, for to you it was given to walk here on earth and at the same time to see your Lord. Your life was holy; and, though no cruel executioner robbed you of it, yet the desire for martyrdom and the sword of compassion pierced your soul a thousand times! As we offer you now our song of praise, O Father, graciously accept it; and since we cannot as yet come to the vision of God, be our advocate before him."

The little poor cell from which Anthony's soul hastened to the beatific vision seems to have retained the atmosphere of his holy death. It has always been held in honor; and it was soon converted into a little chapel. In more recent times a large and beautiful church has been built around it.

The friars decided it would be better not to make Anthony's death known immediately. They were aware of the great veneration which the people had for him, and feared they would not be able to carry out Anthony's dying wish. The crowds would be sure to surge around them and make it quite impossible for them to take the body of the Saint to Padua. But what they tried to keep secret was suddenly made known to all; for, groups of children unaccountably began to run through the streets of Padua, crying: "The holy father is dead; St. Anthony is dead!" The people of the city, who were deeply attached to Anthony, immediately left their work and came like swarms of bees to Arcella, to see their beloved preacher once more. The effect of the announcement by the children was even worse than what the friars had feared. When the men and women of Padua and the neighboring town of Capo di Ponte, to which Arcella belonged, descended upon the little friary and caught sight of the lifeless body of the Saint, they gave vent to their sorrow by tears and wails; but it did not take long and a fight commenced over the body! While the friars of Arcella wished to fulfill the last wish of the Saint and transfer the body to the friary in Padua, the Poor Clares pleaded that, since Anthony had never visited them while he was alive, they should at least possess him in death. The citizens of Arcella and Capo di Ponce were of the same mind, and soon declared they would take up arms to enforce their demand that the burial take place at Arcella.

Meanwhile the brothers had come from Padua, to take the body of St. Anthony to their friary, which he had loved in life and had chosen as his resting-place in death. Again the inhabitants of Capo di Ponte made it clear that they would use armed force to prevent the transfer of the body to Padua. Finally the dispute was taken for settlement to the bishop of Padua, Jacopo Corrado, who listened to the Friars Minor from Padua as well as the Poor Clares, and then decided that the body was to be taken to the friary in Padua. While these negotiations were being carried on, however, the inhabitants of Capo di Ponte, under the pretext of wishing to see Anthony once more, broke down the bolted doors of the friary at Arcella and began to make preparations to take the body away. Fortunately the friars succeeded in dissuading them from carrying out their plan. But since it was very hot and there seemed to be no prospect that the affair would be settled quickly, the friars placed the body in a wooden coffin.

The bishop's verdict soon met with open opposition; and this opposition grew stronger and bolder with the approach of June 17, the date set by the bishop for the transfer. The people of Capo di Ponte occupied the only bridge over the river; and when a temporary bridge of boats was built, they quickly destroyed it with axes. Armed citizens were then drawn up on both sides of the bridge, ready for a battle when the Podesta of Padua resorted to a ruse. He invited the leading men of Capo di Ponte to the Palazzo della Ragione to discuss the matter with him, and then had them interned for a day. Meanwhile the bishop together with his clergy brought Anthony's body back to his beloved Padua. The procession was joined by an immense throng of people who carried burning torches and sang hymns of praise. At the church of the friars the bishop celebrated a solemn Mass, and then the body of the Saint was laid to rest in the church itself.

Luke Belludi, who had been the constant companion of Anthony since his return to Italy, and his beloved friend and disciple throughout his preaching apostolate, remained so attached to the Saint that later on he was called "Brother Luke of St. Anthony." Subsequently St. Anthony appeared to him in a vision (the subject of a painting by Filippo da Verona), in which the Saint told his companion that the city of Padua would soon be freed from the oppression of Ezzelino. In the painting, Luke Belludi is represented as praying at the grave of the Saint in the Basilica, while the city itself is menaced by the forces of Ezzelino; and above, Anthony appears in the clouds, predicting the liberation of the city.

The little church of Santa Maria in Padua where St. Anthony was buried in 1231 had been placed in the care of the Franciscans only two years earlier. However, in 1232 it was torn down, and on its site the building of the great Basilica of St. Anthony was begun, to be completed only a century later. The Lombard-Gothic chapel of this basilica occupies the site of the older church and burial-place of the Saint. In this chapel one can still see at the present day the stone sarcophagus in which the body was placed at the first burial. The inscription on it reads as follows: "Here, during the first years after his death, rested the body of St. Anthony." When the present chapel of St. Anthony was built on the other side of the nave and the relics of the Saint were transferred to the new tomb in it, the old sarcophagus, which now serves as the altar table in the other chapel, was used for Luke Belludi, the friend and associate of Anthony. This we learn from a second inscription which reads: "Then it was used for his companion, the Blessed Luke, until the year 1771." When Luke died about the year 1285, the chapel which he himself had chosen for Anthony thus became his own, and it was henceforth known as the "Capella del Beato Luca Belludi." As these friends of God were united in life and traveled together to preach God's word, so they remained close to each other also after death.

Immediately after his death, Anthony became the object of an extraordinary devotion; and miracle followed miracle, as the prayers of the sick and the afflicted were answered by sudden cures and other wonders. This set on foot a great wave of enthusiasm, and drew large crowds to his tomb, who began to honor him as a Saint even before the pope had canonized him. Often orderly processions were formed; and these were led sometimes by the bishop of Padua and his clergy. The leading knights of the city and the students of the university also took part; and all carried candles of great size. Sometimes the candles were so large that it took sixteen men to carry one of them; and these had to be left outside, because there was no room for them in the church.

Scarcely a month after Anthony's burial, the bishop and clergy and the podesta with his nobles sent messengers to Rome to petition Gregory IX to enroll Anthony among the saints. They gave as reasons the holiness of his life, the great veneration given to him after death, and the many miracles at his tomb. Though the Pope himself was delighted with the glory which God had heaped on his servant, he submitted the petitions of the bishop and city of Padua to the cardinals for consideration. The cardinals in turn appointed a local commission to investigate and report in detail on the wonders which occurred at the tomb. The depositions of the witnesses were so impressive that the pope agreed to proceed with the canonization, and announced it would take place at Spoleto on May 30, 1232.

SAINT OF THE WHOLE WORLD

On the morning of the day appointed, the pope, clothed in festive attire, entered the Cathedral of Spoleto in the company of many cardinals, bishops, and secular princes. In the presence of these ecclesiastical dignitaries and an immense throng of people, the results of the investigation were made known and a list of the miracles which Anthony had worked at his tomb were read. The merits of his holy life were likewise proclaimed to all in a fitting manner. Then the pope rose from his throne with evident signs of joy, lifted his hands to heaven, and enrolled Anthony in the catalog of the saints, selecting as his feast day the day of his death, June 13. Then, as the bells rang out joyfully, the pope intoned a solemn Te Deum to give thanks to God. When the Ambrosian hymn was finished, the pope was so overcome by joy and emotion that he enthusiastically intoned the antiphon of the breviary, *O Doctor optime*, and thus, even at this early date, saluted Anthony as a doctor of the Church: "O excellent doctor, light of Holy Church, blessed Anthony! Lover of God's law, be our advocate with God's Son!"

A few days later, a papal bull announced the canonization of Anthony of Padua to the whole world: "Gregory, Bishop, Servant of the Servants of God, to the venerable brethren, the archbishops and bishops, and to the beloved sons, abbots, priors, and other prelates of the Church: health and apostolic benediction.

"Since the Lord says through the prophet: I will give you to all the people unto praise and glory and honor, and through himself promises that the just will shine forth like the sun in the sight of God, it is pious and just that those whom God crowns and honors in heaven because of their merit and holiness we should honor and glorify on earth by our prayers and veneration, since it is he more truly whom we praise and glorify in them, he who is worthy of praise and glorious forever in his saints. That he may indeed manifest most wonderfully the might of his power and mercifully effect the work of our salvation, he often gives to his faithful ones, whom he always crowns in heaven, honors also here on earth, by performing signs and wonders unto their glorification. In this way he wills to confound the evil of heresy, and to strengthen the true Catholic belief. The faithful are led to rise from their tepidity and are aroused to zeal for good works; the unbelievers are made to banish the darkness and blindness in which they walk and are led back to the right way; and even the Jews and pagans see the true light and turn to Christ, who is the Light, the Way, the Truth, and the Life.

"Wherefore, beloved Sons, We give thanks (if not as much as We should, at least as much as We can) to the Giver of all graces, that in Our days, to the confirmation of the Catholic Faith, and to the confusion of heretical depravity, he has visibly worked new signs and revealed once more the might of his power, thus giving new glory to those who on earth had strengthened the Catholic faith by their whole-hearted service, their words, and their holy deeds. Among these is the blessed Anthony of holy memory, of the Order of Friars Minor, who while on earth possessed great merits, and now living in heaven is glorified by many

94

miracles, and whose holiness is proved by these evident signs . . .

"Although final perseverance alone is sufficient for anyone to be a saint with God in the Church Triumphant (for the Lord says: Be faithful unto death, and I will give you the crown of life), nevertheless, to be considered a saint by those who belong to the Church Militant, two things are necessary: namely, virtues and miracles. These must mutually bear witness to each other, since neither merits without miracles nor miracles without merits fully suffice to prove to men the holiness of anyone. But when genuine virtues precede and evident miracles follow, we possess sure signs of holiness which induce us to venerate him whom God by such merits and signs bids us honor . . .

"By the advice then of our brethren, the cardinals, and of all the prelates dwelling at the papal court, we have decreed to enroll in the catalog of the saints Anthony, who after his days on earth has merited to be with Christ in heaven; lest We should seem in any way to withhold from him the honor and glory due him, were We any longer to leave him without the veneration of men whom God has so honored in heaven. Because therefore, according to the word of the Gospel, men do not light a lamp and put it under the measure, but upon the lamp-stand, so as to give light to all in the house, and because the lamp of this Saint has shone so brilliantly that by God's grace it has merited to be put, not under the measure, but upon the lamp-stand, We beseech all of you, admonish you most earnestly, and bid you through this apostolic writing to incite the pious faithful to honor him for their own salvation, to celebrate his feast, and cause it to be celebrated, each year on the thirteenth of June, that the Lord moved by his prayers may grant us grace in the present life and glory in that to come. Wishing further that the tomb of this great Confessor, who through the light of his miracles sheds luster on the whole Church, be fittingly honored and visited, We, confiding in the mercy of God and the authority of the blessed Apostles Peter and Paul, grant to all who, truly penitent and confessed, shall with due reverence visit it on his feast or during the octave, an indulgence of one year of the penance imposed upon them.

"Given at Spoleto, on the eleventh of June, in the sixth year of Our pontificate."

HONORED BY THE WHOLE WORLD

The people of Padua, who were attached to Anthony by a singular love, gave their great Saint a lasting memorial in the magnificent basilica which they erected. The cornerstone was laid in the same year in which he was canonized. Work, indeed, slowed down in the years 1237 to 1256, when Padua lay prostrate under the tyranny of Ezzelino; but once the city was free from his yoke, the building progressed anew. Some hundred years were required to complete the magnificent edifice, built in the Byzantine-Gothic, and in part purely Gothic, style. To the pilgrim it seems almost as though Padua had tried by means of this large and beautiful structure to surpass Assisi's tribute to St. Francis. Its general plan has the form of a cross, some 390 feet in length and 180 feet in width. Exteriorly, its eight cupolas and two slender bell-towers form a fascinating silhouette against the Italian skies. Inside, the visitor is entranced by the variety of paintings and mosaics, the diversity of chapels, and the tremendous thrust of the walls, though he may be disconcerted perhaps by the general lack of artistic unity. Near the plain high altar with Donatello's Crucifixion group is the burial chapel of St. Anthony, which in its present lines follows plans made in the sixteenth century. It is the beauty-spot of the basilica, and a favorite place of prayer for the pilgrims. The stone sarcophagus containing the bones of the Saint forms its altar, to which one ascends on some seven steps. The pilgrims, however, when they wish to venerate the grave of the Saint, usually go behind the altar where they can come close to the tomb. There they stand and pray with their right hand resting against the side of the tomb.

At first the remains of the Saint rested in the chapel opposite, as we have related. Then, in April, 1263, when construction of the basilica had reached the transept, the Senate of Padua decreed that the body of St. Anthony should be transferred to the new church. Present at the translation was Friar Bonaventure, then minister general of the order, who himself was later on canonized and made a doctor of the Church. When the coffin was opened (thirty two years after Anthony's death), only the bones of his body remained except for his tongue which was preserved intact. At the sight of this miracle, Bonaventure exclaimed in awe: "O blessed tongue, you have always praised the Lord and led others to praise him! Now we can clearly see how great indeed have been your merits before God!" A second transfer took place in 1310, when the middle aisle of the church was completely finished. The bones received their last resting place in the year 1350, when the present chapel and its tomb were completed. This translation took place in the presence of Cardinal Guido de Montfort, great-grandson of St. Louis IX of France. On a journey to Cuges the cardinal had fallen seriously ill, and had made the vow that if he recovered he would assist personally at the transfer of the Saint to the new chapel, and obtain for the city of Cuges a relic of the Wonderworker. He conscientiously fulfilled both promises.

Art has honored Anthony not only in the masterpieces that adorn the basilica, but also in the Capella del Tesoro (Relic-chapel or Treasury), which at the end of the seventeenth century, in the hey-day of Baroque, was erected in place of the earlier chapel of the Stigmata, and now con-

97

tains many precious relics and souvenirs of the Saint. In addition, art has constantly chosen Anthony as a subject for painting, sculpture, and other media. Rather than lose ourselves in the details of these innumerable pieces, it is more instructive to turn to the symbols which have been given to St. Anthony down through the centuries.

The first of these, one which Anthony has almost invariably retained through the years, is the book. The question whether this is to be taken as a symbol of prayer or of wisdom is answered by the oldest representations of the Saint, since in them the open book carries the words of Holy Scripture: "I pleaded, and the spirit of wisdom and understanding came to me." But since in the course of time the book was used for other Franciscan teachers as well, it ceased to be Anthony's distinguishing mark. Hence he received other symbols which indicated his connection with the Augustinian Canons and St. Augustine himself: the glowing flame, the burning heart, or the heart alone. Since the fifteenth century he is made to carry the lily, symbol of a life of purity and complete dedication to God; and from the sixteenth century, the cross with or without a corpus. While the cross with the image of Christ would stand for the Saint's love for the Passion of Christ, the bare cross would be either the sign of the preacher or, as it is also used for Anthony the Abbot, a symbol of the hermit's life.

The most popular statue of St. Anthony today is the one which shows him with the Child Jesus. Yet this is a late addition, appearing for the first time only in 1439, which makes it more or less contemporary with the legend that the Child appeared to the Saint. At first, this symbol was meant to portray Anthony as the "Herald of the Incarnate Word," as he was aptly called, because the Child appears originally as motionless, or as a tiny figure on the breast or the book of the Saint; and in two representations Anthony is clothed as an Augustinian Canon. Only gradually did the Child appear to be talking familiarly with the Saint, in keeping with the well-known legend: one day as Anthony was at prayer in a certain city, the divine Child appeared to him. Anthony took him into his arms and gazed in rapture upon his holy face. This scene was observed by Anthony's host; but the Saint demanded of him the promise to remain silent about the vision during his lifetime.

The changing interpretation of St. Anthony in art reflects a like concept on the part of the literature of the Middle Ages on the Saint. Yet even the later legends, which have transformed Anthony the miracle-worker after his death into a wonderworker during his life, cannot completely obscure the true picture of the Saint. One of them, in fact, strikingly describes his character: "What Peter was to the Church, that Francis was to the Seraphic Order: founder, leader, and shepherd; and what Paul was to the Church; that Anthony was to the order: preacher, teacher, and doctor."

Even more true and exact than the foregoing is the picture of Anthony contained in the liturgical cult bestowed on him by the Roman Breviary and the Roman Missal. When Gregory IX, at the end of the canonization ceremony, intoned the antiphon for a Doctor of the Church, he had no intention of officially enrolling St. Anthony among her Teachers (at that time, in fact, only four doctors were recognized: Ambrose, Augustine, Jerome, and Gregory the Great, all of whom belonged to Christian antiquity). Neither did the books of the Roman liturgy imply this when they chose for Anthony's Mass and Office the texts used for a doctor: in the Missal, the Introit "In the midst of the assembly has the Lord opened his mouth," the Gospel "You are the salt of the earth," and the Credo; or in the Breviary, the eighth responsory at Matins, "In the midst," and the Magnificat-antiphon, "O excellent Doctor, Light of Holy Church." The liturgy, undoubtedly inspired and influenced by Gregory IX, whose convictions it reflects, merely indicated that Anthony deserved to be honored as a wonderful preacher, teacher, and writer.

It was in this form that the liturgical cult of St. Anthony was spread far and wide in the fourteenth, fifteenth, and sixteenth centuries; for, it was through the influence of the Franciscan Order that the liturgical books of the Roman See came to be generally adopted. The liturgical reform of Pope St. Pius V abolished the feast of St. Anthony along with many others, though it was retained with the old formulas in the Franciscan Order and in the countries of Portugal and Brazil. It was soon restored to the whole Church by Sixtus V in 1585, but was now given the formulary of a simple Confessor. As a result, until 1946, when Pius XII declared Anthony a Doctor, the liturgical honors paid the Saint in the order and in Portugal and Brazil differed from those of the rest of the Catholic Church.

Popular devotion followed an entirely different path almost immediately after Anthony's death, when the people came to his tomb to pray for every need of soul and body and were heard. Encouraged by such a response, the people soon imagined that Anthony had been a wonder-worker also during life and an extraordinary helper in every need. Although many were healed at the grave of St. Francis in Assisi, the Father and Patriarch of the Seraphic Order was never the object of such devotion as Anthony, his son and disciple, received from the people. To them the latter became simply "Il Santo," which Leo XIII once interpreted as "the Saint of the whole world." Anthony has been adopted as heavenly patron for priests, for children, and for engaged couples. In times of war and pest, in every danger, and in the battle against the powers of darkness, men look to him as a special patron. He is likewise invoked as a vigilant protector for letters, and for travelers on sea and land. Above all, many have recourse to him when they have lost anything and confidently hope to find it again through his intercession. Yet there is little or nothing in the actual historical facts of his life on which to base such devotions. Some arise from miracles he wrought after his death, but just as many seem to have their foundation in purely legendary stories. It is perhaps unfortunate that Anthony, who in his lifetime gave himself wholly to the service of the Church and was before all else God's instrument for the salvation of souls, should become to such a great extent the patron saint whose help is sought in earthly needs!

The Church, however, has corrected this distortion of his true image in the veneration of the faithful and has set forth once more his real greatness and his spiritual role, inasmuch as she has restored, as it were, and solemnly confirmed the ancient veneration of St. Anthony as a Doctor and Teacher, the Servant of the Gospel and the Church.

MADE A DOCTOR OF THE CHURCH

Rejoice, happy Portugal! Happy Padua, be glad! For the one has given to earth, the other to heaven, a man not unlike a brilliant star—for not only by the holiness of his life and the fame of his miracles, but also by the radiant splendor of heavenly doctrine, he has illumined the whole world and even now sheds upon it a brilliant light . . .

How much light Anthony shed upon the world by his doctrine and by his preaching of the divine word, is attested by his contemporaries no less than by the men of our day. They bestow the highest praise on his wisdom, and extol to the skies his sacred eloquence. To him, in truth, who reads the sermons of Padua's Saint, Anthony is revealed as most skilled in Sacred Scripture, as a remarkable theologian of the teachings of our Faith, and as an exceptional teacher and master in ascetical and mystical subjects.

All this is like a treasury of divine oratory, and can provide abundant and rich material especially for the preachers of the Gospel. It constitutes likewise a rich armory from which sacred orators in particular can draw an abundance of solid arguments to defend the truth, combat errors, refute heresies, and draw back to the right way those who have gone astray. But because Anthony most frequently uses texts and phrases drawn from the Gospel, he rightly and justly appears worthy of the title "Doctor of the Gospel." From him indeed, as from a perennial fountain of living water, not a few doctors, theologians, and preachers of the divine word have constantly drawn and continue to draw abundantly, since they esteem him as their master and consider him a Teacher of holy Church.

In Italy especially did his apostolic power and zeal become famous, for here he undertook his most exhausting labors, though we can not forget his great work in many provinces of France. Indeed, the zeal for souls he possessed led Anthony to embrace all, without discrimination of race or country: the Portuguese, Africans, Italians, French—and all in fact whom he found in need of the Catholic truth. Against the heretics of that day, the Albigensians, Cathari, and Patarines, so numerous at that period and so intent on extinguishing the light of the true faith in the hearts of the faithful, Anthony strove so mightily and so successfully that he merited to be called the "Hammer of Heretics." Not to be passed over, but to be considered of greatest value, is the high praise which Pope Gregory IX paid to the Saint of Padua when he called him the "Ark of the Testament" and the "Repository of Holy Scripture." It is very noteworthy too that when Gregory IX canonized Anthony on May 30, 1232, hardly eleven months after his death, tradition says the pope concluded by intoning in a joyful voice the antiphon of a Doctor: "O most excellent Doctor, light of Holy Church, Blessed Anthony, lover of the divine law, pray for us to the Son of God." . . .

Declaration of Pius XII

Therefore we willingly and gladly accede to the petitions of all the Franciscans and other petitioners, and by these letters present, in sure knowledge and after mature deliberation, with the fulness of Our apostolic power, We constitute and declare St. Anthony of Padua, Confessor, a Doctor of the universal Church. Any constitutions and apostolic ordinances or anything else whatever which might oppose this have no force. We order and decree that these present letters are always to be authentic, valid, and effective; that they are endowed with and have their full and complete effect; that thus they must be interpreted and defined; that, if perchance anything concerning this matter other than is contained in these letters is attempted by any authority whatsoever, either knowingly or unknowingly, it is henceforth invalid and groundless.

Given at Rome at St. Peter's, under the ring of the Fisherman, on January 16, the Feast of the Franciscan Protomartyrs, 1946, in the seventh year of our Pontificate.

CHRONOLOGICAL TABLE

Battle at Ourique	1139
Afonso I, king of Portugal	1139-1185
Second Crusade	1147-48
Sancho I, king of Portugal	1185-1211
Birth of Fernando (Anthony)	1195
Innocent III	1198-1216
Suger I, bishop of Lisbon	d. 1209
Suger II Viegas, bishop of Lisbon	1209-1232
Oral confirmation of the rule	1210 (1209)
Fernando becomes an Augustinian at São Vicente	about 1210
Peter, bishop of Coimbra	1210-1231
Afonso II, king of Portugal	1211-1239
Transfer of Fernando to Santa Cruz	1212 (1211)
Stephen Soares de Silva, bishop of Braga	1211-1239
Battle at Las Navas	1212 (July 16)
Fourth Lateran Council	1215 (Nov.)
Arrival of the Franciscans in Portugal	1217
Honorius III	1216-1227
Simon de Sully, archbishop of Bourges	1218-1232
Second mission of the Franciscans	1219
Protomartyrs in Morocco	1220 (Jan. 16)
Novitiate in the Franciscan Order	since 1220 (Sept. 22)
Chapter at the Porziuncola	1221 (May 30)
Anthony as a hermit in Montepaolo	1221-1222

Ricciardellus Belmonti, bishop of Forli	1221-1225
Anthony's sermon at Forli	1222 (summer)
First period of preaching (Anthony in Italy)	1222-1224
Appointed lector by St. Francis	about 1223
Second period of preaching (Anthony in France)	1224-1227
Chapter at Arles	1224 (Sept. 29)
Sermon at the Synod of Bourges	1225 (Nov. 30)
Death of St. Francis	1226 (Oct. 3)
Sermon in the church-yard at Limoges	1226 (Nov. 2)
Generalate of John Parenti	1227-1232
Gregory IX	1227-1241
Third period of preaching (in Italy)	1227-1231
Composition of the Sunday Sermons	1228
Canonization of St. Francis	1228 (July 16)
Translation of St. Francis at Assisi	1230 (May 25)
Quo elongati: Declaration of Gregory IX	1230 (Sept. 28)
Year of peace in the March of Treviso	1230-1231
Composition of Feastday Sermons	1230-1231 (winter)
Lenten Sermons of St. Anthony	1231 (Feb. 5-April 23)
Debtors' decree at Padua	1231 (March 15)
Appeal of Anthony to Ezzelino	1231 (after Lent)
Anthony in the hermitage of Camposampiero	1231 (after his appeal)
Death of St. Anthony	1231 (June 13)
Canonization	1232 (May 30)
Declared a Doctor of the Church	1946 (Jan. 16)